A CIP catalogue record for this book is available from the British Library

ISBN   0 9527638 3 4

Designed, printed and bound by MFP Design & Print, Stretford, Manchester M32 0JT. Telephone: 0161 864 4540.

Published by FIDO PUBLISHING, Appleby-in-Westmorland, Cumbria CA16 6BD.

VILLAGE CRICKET

The genuine article

Words by Gordon Thorburn

Photographs by John Baxter

Foreword by David Byas

Illustrations by Anna Frances

Acknowledgements are gratefully made to:

the teams — the boys and men who were members of, and who played against, the following: Scarborough High School for Boys 2nd XI, 1962/63; Seamer CC 1962/64; Perivale CC 1968; Bungay CC 1987/88; New Inn pub team, Hoff, 1992/93;

all umpires everywhere;

AND ABOVE ALL, thanks go to those who played for and against Harleston CC, Norfolk, likewise The Cherry Tree pub team, Harleston, in the years between 1975 and 1990; and to those brave men of Staffield CC of Kirkoswald, Cumbria, and their opponents, who allowed themselves to be photographed without really knowing why.

Also to the editors of the *Diss Express* and the *South Norfolk News* in the 1970s and 80s, in whose newspapers some of the cricket in this book was first described. Also to Robert Cockroft who, as Features Editor of the *Yorkshire Post*, allowed some of the characters and mysteries of the North Dales Triangle to be first brought to light.

The scoreboard reads:

TOTAL
LAST MAN
HOME
VISITORS

Foreword

Could anyone really argue but that village cricket is the foundation on which the game we all love so much is built?

Like many of my fellow Yorkshire County professionals, I was introduced to the game through my involvement with the local club side which, in summer, is invariably the focal point of sporting activity. At these village clubs, the dedicated enthusiasts don't just play in and captain the teams. They also have to share in the non-glamorous side of cricket, preparing and rolling the pitches, maintaining the ground, doing the teas and taking on all the other small jobs which are essential in making village cricket happen.

These enthusiasts also have the welfare of budding young cricketers at heart, instilling in them the necessary skills and virtues and above all the enjoyment of playing the game.

The great reward is the satisfaction of seeing these young players progress into the first team. The more talented ones may move up to a better standard of cricket, and maybe on towards their ultimate ambition of playing for a County side.

Two of England's finest ever all-rounders, Wilfrid Rhodes and George Herbert Hirst (both Yorkshiremen!!) were products of the same village team in the Huddersfield League. Of course, the characters that Gordon Thorburn writes about are probably not *quite* as good as that . . .

David Byas, Captain,
Yorkshire County Cricket Club
April 1996

Preface & Dedication

This book is about a season — the 64th, or possibly the 89th, or it could have been the 113th — in the patchy history of Garthrigg How Cricket Club. The village is in the Yorkshire Dales and the team plays its Saturday cricket in Division 3 of the Nippon Missionary 4WD Fellside League. On Sundays it's cup matches and friendlies.

It's all real cricket, and basic cricket. It has nothing to do with Test matches and stars and playing for your life. These lads do it because they like doing it and for no other reason.

Everyone who ever played or watched village cricket will recognise the cricket in this book, because it's all true. Everything that happens in Garthrigg How's season, did happen. I know, because I was there.

My wife Sue, at a time when our family was very young and there were many, many more important things to do than play cricket all day, never once said a complaining word.

If it's any consolation for all those summer weekends which could have been better spent, then let me dedicate this book to her.

I don't think many would argue but that my writing was always of more value than my cricket, and so here we have something come out of it at last... *To Sue.*

Gordon Thorburn
January 1996

Part One

BEFORE THE DINNER, THE DINNER, AND AFTER THE DINNER

Spring has come to the North Dales Triangle, that small but regularly shaped piece of Paradise which you can just about identify as Upper Cronkleydale if you search the overlap between OS Landranger sheets 92 and 98.

Spring! Watery sunshine, bright colours, and hope. While cricket bats are being adjudged capable of one more season, and whole households are being forced to search high and low for that little key thing Dad needs to get the old flattened studs out of his cricket boots, Springtime strangers to the Triangle will stop and stare at the more obvious signs of country life.

Up there, near the top of the dale, is the market town of Cronkley, not much different from itself of 150 years ago because it's too small and remote for a supermarket. You will find a main street and market square with two greengrocers, two butchers, two cafés, and a chemist's where the elderly pharmacist still makes up bygone remedies like lead and opium mixture for swollen joints.

There are two fish and chip shops, five pubs and The Langdon Arms, a hotel with two stars and three bars, including one at the back where farmers go in their boots.

H Bigney & Son, Agricultural Engineers, is also the garage, feed store and ironmonger, in which shop can be found every useful non-food and non-pharmaceutical item in the known universe apart from cloth caps, carpets, corsets and crêpe de Chine, all of which are obtainable at Stacey & Belderson. The Moot Hall stands in the middle of the market square. The best view of it for a picturesque photograph is from the doorway of the Chow Fan take-away.

Cronkley is the apex of the North Dales Triangle, while the base is marked further down in slightly wider pastures by the villages of Garthrigg How and Great Cubberthwaite.

Garthrigg How is locally well known for Belinda Smailes, who rules with sarcastic warmth at The Wintering Hogg Inn. The snug bar is where the cricket teams get their tea. Also well known is Lady Marjory, Marchioness of Keld, gracious and eccentric occupant of Garthrigg Hall,

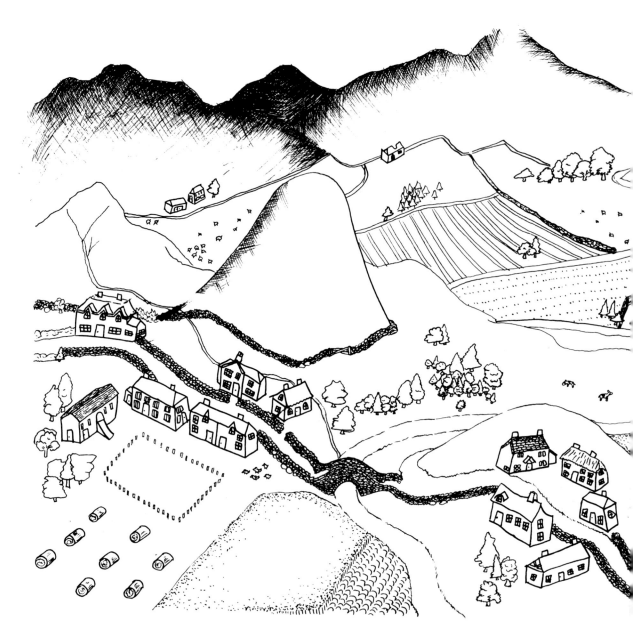

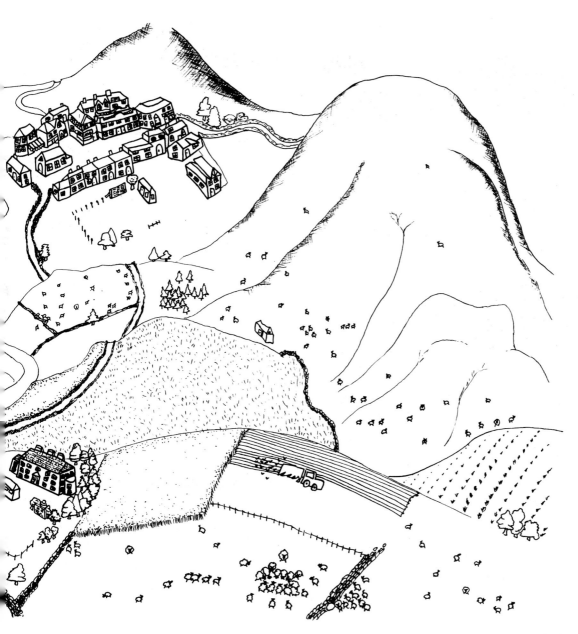

whose reputation rests, like Belinda's, on the sharpness of her wit, but also on her aristocratic ability to drink any mortal under the table.

The old Marquis, that is Lady Marjory's late husband's grandfather, was very keen on cricket and had his gardeners cut a square within sight of his main drawing room, so that the Gentlemen of the North Riding could play the touring Australians in 1920-something. It is on this hallowed ground that Garthrigg How CC now plays.

Great Cubberthwaite, as any resident of Cronkley or Garthrigg How will tell you, isn't well known for anything at all, and vice versa, but you won't find a better pint anywhere than at The Rough Lamb. This ancient and frill-less public house stands just outside the village, below Cubberstones, where rises Cubberthwaite Beck before it races down the dale side to join the River Cronk at New Saint Cuthbert's Bridge.

Standing on the new bridge, which is 300 years old and just wide enough for a tractor, you can look, as St Cuthbert did, westerly up the dale towards Cronkley and see the narrowing, rising green valley with its limestone, drystone walls and dotted barns disappearing into higher, bluer hills.

Look to the south side and you'll see Stemnetting Pike, a symmetrical cone of a hill in among all this irregular rise and fall and elevated flat top. Look up to the north and you'll feel slightly shivery about the looming mass of Blood Fell, one of the highest Pennines. Everybody local goes up Blood Fell once in their lives, forced there by their primary school teacher. A farmer might go up a couple of times a year with the little black and white dog to gather any mad sheep. Otherwise the rambling visitors have it to themselves.

St Cuthbert commanded two trees to lie down across the River Cronk to make a bridge for him. All you have to do now, standing on this miraculous spot, is decide whether to have a pint and a home-cured ham sandwich for your lunch at The Rough Lamb, or a pint and a Chicken Kiev with rice or chips at The Wintering Hogg.

First, one more little look around. There might be cloud and shadow on Blood Fell top but there's sunlight and grass being cut on Great

Cubberthwaite cricket field just across the road from you. At Cronkley CC, if you did but know, scoreboard numbers are being repainted by the wicket-keeper's wife in the vain hope that this will get her out of doing the teas.

Garthrigg How's skipper Wayne Satterdyke has just gone into the changing hut for the first time this year. He has found Barry Naylor's kit, left there all winter, and there is a mouse's nest in the jockstrap.

But we get ahead of ourselves. Before you can follow the season to come with understanding and sympathy, you need to know what went on at the end of the previous season, and even a little bit before that. In fact, three years before we begin, disbandment had been on the agenda at the Garthrigg How CC AGM. Belinda Smailes, AKA the She-Dragon, was on the brink of tears as aged Club President Ashley Broadhurst, later to die so famously in a trombone accident, asked for the fourth time for a volunteer to captain the side.

There was animated conversation at the table known in Belinda's food-waitressing code as Dartboard Two. Wayne Satterdyke, Garthrigg How native and resident but a teacher up at Cronkley Church of England Primary School, was heard to say that he wouldn't, his refusal being embroidered with words which were surely inappropriate for an associate member of the C of E.

Nevertheless his name went forward and he was immediately appointed. Few of the old committee wanted to serve again, so Satterdyke took rapid revenge and got everybody sitting at Dartboard Two on the new committee.

Over the next couple of years some of the classier players went off to Richmond and Barnard Castle in search of the myth of better cricket, and their places were taken by more enthusiastic, more comradely but less capable men. There was a consequent rise in the takings at The Wintering Hogg on match days, and an equal and opposite decline in the percentage of matches won.

As we come towards the end of the season preceding the one about to start, Garthrigg How's team found itself facing what skipper Satterdyke called "a do or die situation". If they did, they would stay up in Division 3 of the league. If they died, they would be relegated.

In precisely the same DOD situation were Garthrigg How's opponents in the last match, Raiswell. The first relegation place was already settled, Shunner Druids having lost to everybody twice. Garthrigg How's only two league wins, and likewise Raiswell's, were thus accounted for. The match between themselves at Raiswell, earlier in the season, had been rained off. Batting and bowling points were exactly even. It was either team's third win which would decide the drop.

So important was this match that two umpires were called up from the North Riding Association pool, and not one Garthrigg How player could be found in any public house after midnight on the Friday. What a match that was! Excitement? Drama? Nerve-tingling, white-knuckling heroism? Not half! Do you remember when Cheyne, the Scottish fast bowler, ran up to . . .

But that was September, end of last season, a sunny, leafy Saturday in history. We'll stop off a while in that November now. The fog is settling thickly in the North Dales Triangle and a small number of cricketers, a larger number of men and youths who play cricket, and a larger still number of wives, girlfriends and non-cricketing guests make their way to The Wintering Hogg Inn for the Garthrigg How Cricket Club Annual Dinner.

Some of them will never forget that glorious day when Raiswell were vanquished and Division 3 status was thus assured for another season. Some of them may even recall the golden words of the match report in the Cronkleydale Mercury. How well that glittering prose had reflected the gleam of a precious victory! Perhaps that magnificent triumph will be mentioned in the speeches tonight. Perhaps not.

The main speaker, of course, was to have been the Club President. Owing to the unfortunate trombone accident already mentioned, the club did not have a President at this moment. It had a stand-in President, or President Pro Tem as he called himself, whose main claim to high office was that he was always in The Wintering Hogg on Saturday nights, when the cricket team was in.

The President Pro Tem, an elderly farmer called Manny Stockdale, saw himself as having three duties once the dinner — minestrone soup, lasagne with chips and salad, chocolate mousse — was over.

The first duty was to propose "The Queen", which he did, thus giving permission to those already smoking.

The second was to review the playing season in his speech, also paying tribute to Ashley Broadhurst, President of many years and last man alive to have played trombone with the High Cronkley Lead Mine Silver Band. The third duty was to welcome the incoming permanent President, Lady Marjory, Marchioness of Keld, Mistress of Garthrigg Hall and captain of The Wintering Hogg fives and threes team.

An unforeseen fourth duty had been to discover the bottom of a bottle of 12-year-old Glenfarclas, success at which prevented the performance of the second and third duties. So it was that the President Pro Tem collapsed, immediately after mentioning the monarch, into a state of suspended animation, his deep and untroubled slumbers punctuated only by an occasional break of wind.

Skipper Wayne Satterdyke, however, was still marginally sober, enough to raise his pint in response to the Loyal Toast. He stood up, stubbed his fag out and declared "Long Live the Republic!".

Then, realising that Manny Stockdale had had it, he tottered over to Lady Marjory carrying a Darlington Co-op carrier bag.

"Wards" he said, swaying as he faced the seated aristocrat across the remains of a very fine mature farmhouse Wensleydale cheese, obtained by Belinda the She-Dragon as part of her continuing support of the dark-green-to-black economy.

"Wards?" inquired My Lady, raising a noble eyebrow.

"Wards. Of Year. Wards. Not captain get ward."

The short and slightly fiery skipper turned after an attempt at a gracious bow which resulted only in him pouring his pint carefully onto the floor, and lurched back to his seat. Gaining it, he beamed expectantly at Lady Marjory, raised his empty glass, tried to get up again, failed, and

shouted his introduction from an ungentlemanly position.

"Order please!" he bawled. "Bessov order! Thangyoh! Play sirence for the Marshnessov Kell. Laysan gennermen. Her Very High Mazty, the Marshness. Thangyoh."

The Marchioness, known and admired everywhere for her resourcefulness, took a quick look inside the carrier bag. Here was assembled a variety of objects, mostly inconsequential, none of them gift wrapped.

She had hoped there might be a list, but there was not. Oh well. She would have to rely on her own extensive knowledge of the well-shuffled assortment which made up the Garthrigg How cricket team.

Lady Marjory, totally up the beck without her fly box, poured a half pint glass full of Bulgarian Merlot, drank it in one, stood, and smiled confidently at her audience.

"A Young Cricketer of the Year," she began, "is usually considered so because he has shown sporting performance beyond that expected from one so inexperienced. I prefer instead to make this award to the cricketer who is best at being young, who is distinguished by the sheer quantity and quality of human youthfulness displayed.

"As one who has watched parts of many matches from my drawing room window, and who is almost always to be found within these walls when the day's cricket is discussed, I feel I am well qualified to judge who has indeed been the first among all his young equals.

"Who, may I ask, has been sick most often in pub car parks? Who has had to be deposited most often on his mother's doorstep in an unco-ordinated state, causing his older and less athletic team-mates to run away after ringing the doorbell?

"Who, despite innumerable attempts, has scored with not a single one of the many, many attentive and synergistic village virgins at away matches?

"Who has proved most likely to fall off his motorbike, most likely to query umpires' decisions, and most likely to accept drinks from his team mates, knowing he has no money in his own pocket to pay them back? Young Cricketer of the Year, Master Richard Walker, if you please."

Richard Walker, a tall, dark, talented but semi-brainless fast bowler, known as The Beast, walked up to receive his award — a packet of three banana flavoured contraceptives — as if all those traits described by Lady Marjory were cardinal virtues.

The Marchioness searched the carrier and pulled out a 10" 78rpm gramophone record. She read the label to herself and began again.

"Old Player of the Year is not an award frequently offered, but it should be. Of course, it is tempting to do it in parallel with Young Player, giving it according to the characteristics associated with oldness, such as being crotchety, bent and wizened, always forgetting to bring cigarettes, never accepting an LBW decision, moving younger fielders about while the captain isn't looking, and forever moaning and groaning about how things are worse now than they were then.

"Unable to find anyone in the club remotely conforming to these criteria, I have decided instead to give Old Player of the Year to Fred "Chuckles" Padgett for his 103 not out against Raiswell in the last match of the season. Fred deserves this award not just for his century. He, despite being able to comment, had he wished, on the sum total of 26 runs amassed by the entire rest of the team, said not a word in the pub all evening. What's more, he even bought a round. Here then, for old Fred, is a monophonic recording of Funeral Music Around The World by the Scottish Undertakers' Federation Pipe Band.

"Now," Lady Marjory continued, after Fred had given his record to his wife to look after, "we come to Best Dressed Player of the Year. Should this go to Barry Banks for his flannels, creamy and baggy, inherited it is said from his grandfather in the certain knowledge that they had been washed once a season ever since the old boy bought them? I have even heard a rumour that a ten shilling note was recently discovered in the turn-ups.

"Or, should we consider Barry Naylor? Those of you, those many, many of you who do not attend Garthrigg How matches, will not have seen the Incident of The Shining Boots.

"Our captain, Satterdyke, that little shortarse there with his eyes

closed, had wanted to upgrade the image of his team and so had removed Naylor's boots from his kitbag after a Sunday game, knowing that the theft would not be discovered because the said kitbag would not be opened again until next Saturday.

"During the week, Satterdyke dipped the boots in Dulux Brilliant White gloss paint and dried them on the washing line.

"The act of going out to field, wearing these boots, much to the consternation and remark of the Man from Mars, Garthrigg How's only regular home supporter, might have earned Naylor this award had he maintained such a high standard throughout the rest of the season.

"However, consistency is all in an award of this nature and so it — the award for Best Dressed Player, in this case the Ladies' Underwear section pulled out of Littlewoods' catalogue — goes to Barry Banks, for reinstating the style of dress obtaining in the days of George Herbert Hirst and, indeed, 'my Hornby and my Barlow long ago'."

You could just hear Fred Padgett above the applause, saying "They were bloody Lancashire, Hornby and Barlow. What's she doing mentioning them? Bloody Lancashire they were."

"Clubman of the Year is always a difficult one," the Marchioness declared loudly, thus stopping Naylor from running an impromptu 'Who's got the biggest?' competition from the pages of Banks' award.

"Too often it is given to someone of limited cricketing ability who does a lot of work for the club off the field, thus earning the gratitude of more talented and lazier colleagues. 'Give this man an award' they cry, 'lest he loose heart and we have to make the sandwiches. Keep him in the team, even if he can't bat or bowl, for without him we might have to put out the boundary markers ourselves!'

"Thus is a Clubman usually defined, and quite erroneously," was my Lady's opinion. "Clubman of the Year should be he who has been inside the most clubs, and there can be only one candidate at Garthrigg How.

"Richard Asquith, promising bat, opening bowler, highly capable but not entirely sensible all-rounder, is making it his business to enter as many clubs as possible in the time available to him before his marriage to a girl from the Trustee Savings Bank.

"This 'clubbing', as it is known, is closely connected with Asquith's personal zoological research project, in which he aims to produce an accurate physio-demographic profile of the young female population of North Yorkshire and Europe, banking and non-banking.

"Apparently his investigations are based on whether a given female is one who (a) likes to say Yes, and (b) likes what she is saying Yes to.

"In order to identify a sufficient quantity of young females, so that his results will be statistically significant, Asquith has been into every club in the region, ranging from the Reeth Badminton Club to the Deep End Rave Dive, Newcastle; from the York Railwaymen's Association Club to the Red For Go-Go, Leeds.

"Asquith has ventured even further afield in his thirst for knowledge, and has been seen entering clubs in Amsterdam and Marbella. He has also been seen leaving the Yellow Dog Club, Hamburg, looking like he would have cried 'Eureka!' if he'd been able to speak.

"In recognition of his tireless and scholarly efforts, Richard Asquith is named Clubman of the Year, receiving this pack of leads for a propelling pencil."

Lady Marjory rummaged in the bottom of her carrier bag for the final award and came out with not one, but two framed copies of a famous quotation. She looked puzzled, and glanced towards Satterdyke questioningly.

Satterdyke, on his second wind and 11th pint, said helpfully "Moment. Extra Moment. Dobberaneric."

Lady Marjory resolved to herself that she would buy three bottles of Bulgarian Merlot when she was finished, drink two of them and kill Satterdyke in a painful way with the third.

She gave the rest of her eager and appreciative audience a glowing smile and searched her Saturday-night taproom memories for whatever it was that Wayne was on about. Somewhere, a light went on.

"Years before Test Match Special thought of its Champagne Moment," she said, "Garthrigg How Cricket Club had a 'Moment of the Year' Award. This award is always the same. It is a quotation, framed in brown passe-partout, from the great comedian Frank Randle:

Tha knows, ah sat on a pound o' butter t'other day. Eee, ah thowt mi boil 'ad burst.

"There was a Sunday afternoon, at Buttle" Her Ladyship continued, "when the opposition were on their heels at 66 for 5, and might have been falling backwards on 36 for 5 had it not been for Dobber Metcalf's repeated misfielding at square leg.

"How many singles were turned into threes and fours that day, only the Great Immortal and Invisible Scorer knows.

"Of course, Dobber was not well. We must point this out. Dobber was not himself that day. Dobber's eyes were but narrow slits, owing to bright Buttle sunshine, Black Sheep Disease and Old Peculier Lag.

"His levels of hand-eye co-ordination, usually comparable with those of any Chinese conjuror or Hungarian tight-rope walker, had been reduced to those of a Blue Faced Leicester ewe on a January morning on top of Blood Fell. He was, to all intents and purposes, dead.

"Your own, your very own Sunday skipper Eric Erickson, produced the Moment Nomination when, displaying his legendary lightning acumen, he noticed that two dozen runs had been leaked in the square leg area. He therefore moved the shovel-pawed Fred Padgett from second slip to a squarish and leggish position, ten yards directly behind Dobber Metcalf.

"This unique field placing, Erickson announced to fielders, batsmen, umpires and spectator, was to be known forever, in honour of the occasion, as Deep Extra Dobber. A letter to Wisden has not produced the hoped for official confirmation of the new placing, but I am pleased to give the last award of the evening, for Moment of the Year, jointly to Dobber Metcalf and Eric Erickson."

Later on, Dobber said Erickson could have it for the first six months, and Erickson put it behind the radiator for safe keeping and forgot about it. Belinda the She-Dragon discovered it, with all its passe-partout frizzled up, five months later when she was spring cleaning.

Garthrigg How CC

President: Ashley Broadhurst
Hon. Fixture Secretary: Mrs Belinda Smailes,
The Wintering Hogg Inn, Fell End Lane,
Garthrigg How, Cronkley, Yorkshire.
Tel: ex directory.

Averages (last season)

Batting (qualification 10 innings)

	runs	inns	no*	HS	av
F Padgett	761	29	2	103*	28.2
R Asquith	696	36	5	59	22.5
D Davies	313	16	1	46	20.9
B Naylor	448	27	4	53	19.5
W Satterdyke	513	30	1	78	17.7
R Parks	505	31	0	37	16.3
J Halliday	431	28	0	49	15.4
F Metcalf	387	29	2	61	14.3
C Cheyne	154	18	4	31	11.0
E Erickson	196	23	2	38	9.3
B Banks	220	34	10	16	9.2
N Murgatroyd	177	31	7	27	7.4
G Cartmell	106	35	17	11*	5.9
R Walker	32	20	5	5*	2.1

Bowling (qualification 10 wickets)

	overs	mdns	runs	wks	av
C Cheyne	362	97	903	65	13.9
B Banks	184	29	687	40	17.2
B Naylor	69	4	282	15	18.8
R Walker	298	41	891	43	20.7
R Asquith	290	67	886	41	21.6
N Murgatroyd	187	22	760	31	24.5
W Satterdyke	64	6	287	11	26.1
E Erickson	55	4	293	10	29.3

Garthrigg How CC

President: Marjory, Marchioness of Keld,
Hon. Fixture Secretary: Mrs Belinda Smailes,
The Wintering Hogg Inn, Fell End Lane,
Garthrigg How, Cronkley, Yorkshire.
Tel: ex directory.

Fixtures (this season)

Sun April 29	Scallion Cup 1st Round: Kirkby Wathwell	A
Sat May 5	High Hutton	A
Sun May 6	Middleham Trophy 1st: Swale Electricity	H
Sat May 12	Nuncotes	A
Sun May 13	Long Asby	A
Sat May 19	Fingby	A
Sun May 20	Middleham Trophy 2nd or Les Cigalles de Harrogate	H
Sat May 27	Gallinglath	H
Sun May 28	Scallion Cup 2nd or Plate 1st	
Sat Jun 2	Sowerby Rudd	H
Sun Jun 3	Perambulators	H
Sat Jun 9	Cronkley	H
Sun Jun 10	Scallion Cup 3rd or Plate 2nd	
Sat Jun 17	Great Cubberthwaite	A
Sun Jun 18	Buttle	H
Sat Jun 24	Barrowmoor	H
Sun Jun 25	Milk Marketers	H
Sat Jun 30	Crosby Hawker	A
Sun Jul 1	Sunbiggin	H
Sat Jul 7	High Hutton	H
Sun Jul 8	Milk Marketers	A
Sat Jul 14	Nuncotes	H
Sun Jul 15	Seamer	A
Sat Jul 21	Fingby	H
Sun Jul 22	Buttle	A
Sat Jul 28	Gallinglath	A
Sun Jul 29	Fellside Young Farmers	H
Sat Aug 4	Sowerby Rudd	A
Sun Aug 5	Ravenstone	H
Sat Aug 11	Cronkley	A
Sun Aug 12	Long Asby	H
Sat Aug 18	Great Cubberthwaite	H
Sun Aug 19	Perambulators	A
Sat Aug 25	Barrowmoor	A
Sun Aug 26	TBA	
Sat Sep 1	Crosby Hawker	H
Sun Sep 2	Darguesby	A
Sun Sep 9	President's XI	H

Part Two

THE SEASON, FIRST HALF

Momentous day for Garthrigg How

It may be that the new season's 'Moment of the Year' Award is already won, since there were no less than two Moments of the highest quality in Sunday's game, the first this year, away to Kirkby Wathwell in Round One of the Scallion Cup.

Rain never stopped play in the Scallion Cup, nor flood nor tempest nor subterranean fire. It's life or death, is the Scallion Cup, and 40 overs a side.

The team transport, Cecil Hardwick's 1972 Bedford minibus, is capable of accelerating to 45mph in ten point nought minutes. It is converted from 12 seats to 14 and departs from where there used to be a gate on The Wintering Hogg car park. In-flight meals are not served and so, as departure time approaches, cricket players make a solid trade for the pub in cold roast brisket and raw onion-ring doorsteps.

Sitting in the back of the Bedford with one of these in his hand, your correspondent contemplated the richly spiced variety of the haircuts of Garthrigg How CC, and the wisdom of agreeing at 12.30am that same day, in that same place from which even now we roared and spluttered, to be umpire in the Scallion Cup.

Kirkby Wathwell's is a diabolical wicket on an 11 degree slope, and the location of each of its stones is known precisely to the home bowlers. In a hot late-April sun after three solid days of rain, Garthrigg How lost the toss and padded up without needing to be asked.

The heads of normal-sized batsmen at the bottom end of the pitch appear to be roughly level with the feet of the bowler as he delivers from the top end, and fast-enough bowler Warren Skeeby took full advantage of this fact, hitting them (the batsmen, not his feet) in many interesting places. Erickson, for instance, played and missed outside his off stump while getting four leg byes off his left buttock, a painful and terminal experience, since exactly the same shot next ball produced only the displacement of middle stump.

At 19 for 4, hitherto undisturbed opening bat Reginald Parks, motoring along on 2 not out, earned the day and the year's first Moment Award Nomination. An especially rapid ball from the competitive and barrel chested Skeeby rose almost vertically from the stone which lies on a length on middle-and-off at the downward end, and hit Parks on the temple.

Dear Reginald waited until he was sure everybody was watching, spun theatrically five times before collapsing to the ground, got up, swayed as in temporary faculty suspension while leaning on his bat, adjusted his box, and was adjudged out 'hit wicket' by your impartial correspondent when his cap fell off and dislodged a bail.

Somehow, and nobody could give a reason, Halliday and Naylor stayed in, battered but not broken, proving that fortune favours the over 40s. Sages in the pavilion agreed that 100 would be a good score on this wicket. Garthrigg How got to 94 all out.

After a tea including Warren Skeeby's mother's monolithic cheese scones, the visitors bowled well and Kirkby Wathwell were struggling at 63 for 5 off 29 overs.

The two big Dicks, Richards Walker and Asquith, were bowling like men threatened with having to sit next to Fred Padgett on the team bus to all away matches that year — as indeed they had been — and 94 wasn't looking so bad.

Garthrigg How's luck now took another turn, or rather a double bend. A wicket fell — 67 for 6 — and a warm welcome was given to the Reverend Norton, chaplain at near-by RAF Scotch Corner, but Sunday captain Erickson was more concerned to see Warren Skeeby padding up. Skeeby was rumoured to be on secret payments from Tony Nicholson's sports shop in Richmond because of the number of new cricket balls he consigned each week to undiscoverable parts. This match, tightly balanced as it was, could be severely tipped if Skeeby came in.

Erickson passed the word. On no account was another wicket to fall, and the Reverend Norton was to keep the strike. This was a Cup game. A draw was not an option, and so Garthrigg How's tactic had to be to slow the scoring, which meant saving RAF Scotch Corner and Kirkby Wathwell's slowest and most reverend cricket player.

Sure enough, the flying proctor obliged with studied defence to five balls an over, then a run off the sixth as everybody, including Garthrigg How's venerable wicket-keeper, fell miles back to allow even the Reverend enough time and space to call "Come one!".

With Asquith and Walker continuing to bowl with ferocity and beastliness, not to mention nagging accuracy, this lasted for four overs. Indeed, it was here that Walker permanently confirmed his status as Team Beast, hitting the Rev Norton in the box with three consecutive deliveries as he backed away to square leg. The local air force's spiritual leader took it all well and so presumably will go on to become a bishop.

It was 71 for 6, four more overs to go, and then we had our second Moment Nominee. Neville Murgatroyd is a well-founded character, about the height of a dry-stone wall and twice as wide, and yet he is noted for his athleticism in the field. He leaps and dives in spectacular attempts at catches, often landing with a force which reminds the better educated among us of Alexander Pope's epitaph for Sir John Vanbrugh, architect of Castle Howard, Blenheim Palace and so on:

> Lie heavy on him, Earth, for he
> Laid many a heavy load on thee.

None of Murgatroyd's catches could have been more gravity-defying and breathtaking than the catch he held now, high, high to his left as he stood at backward point. It was taken off a slash of a cut shot that would otherwise have gone for four, first bounce.

This catch was all the more remarkable because the shot came, as a complete surprise, from the Reverend Norton, he of the undivided collar and single mind.

Murgatroyd returned to earth upright from his haddock-like leap,

his hands firmly together in front of his chest, clasping the ball. He looked towards his skipper for congratulations.

Instead, he received The Look. Instantly reminded of his skipper's instructions — no wicket must fall — with a shocked and ghastly cry the dismayed Murgatroyd extended his arm as if signalling to turn right and dropped the ball on the grass where, had it been as hot as Murgatroyd made out, it would have started a fire.

This had been the last ball of the over and Murgatroyd's noble, unselfish action in dropping his catch was to prove worthless. The Reverend's partner snicked the next past third man for four, then ran out the Reverend, and in came Warren Skeeby, on strike.

Skeeby took a short while — four forward prods completely missing invisible cricket balls — to decide that his usual policy, known as Shine or Bust, had better be applied. The game was finished in a few minutes with Skeeby's final six, a top edge into the churchyard, giving Kirkby Wathwell a more than adequate margin.

Garthrigg How 94, Naylor 25, Halliday 21. Skeeby 5-11.
Kirkby Wathwell 99-7, Skeeby 24 n.o. Walker 4-41, Asquith 3-47.

Garthrigg How play Great Cubberthwaite in the Scallion Plate, first round, on Sunday May 28, at home.

SATURDAY MAY 5

Garthrigg How go long way for nothing

The thought of another lengthy Saturday journey in Cecil Hardwick's 1972 Bedford minibus, only one careful owner, is always enough to make the entire Garthrigg How team look like Fred Padgett when it's his round. When you add that the journey in question will be to High Hutton, not one but two hills and dales away, a place where the sheep bite the dogs and Garthrigg How victories are as rare as unicorn droppings, you will understand why faces were long and few words were spoken in the car park of The Wintering Hogg.

One of the longest faces belonged to your correspondent, he having been informed the previous evening — in that very same place of resort — that he had been unanimously elected by the Garthrigg How CC Committee to be Life Umpire and Vice President.

Such a vote of confidence, like Erickson's King George VI tossing florin, has two sides but one side usually falls uppermost.

Even a selection of Lady Marjory's jokes — she was in the pub for a lunchtime Mah Jongg session with Belinda the She-Dragon and any two innocent tourists — could not raise a titter, not even the one about the all-female orchestra playing at Catterick Camp.

Satterdyke and Erickson, the usual captains, had been unable to break previous engagements; the High Hutton skipper Gorman hadn't got a coin; and so it was surrogate skipper Banks who searched his capacious flannel pockets for the aforementioned tossing florin, KGVI, 1948, loaned to him with dire threats by his Sunday leader and now loaned to Gorman.

Obviously our Barry had something exotic planned for supper. To ensure he was on time for it he called tails, won (of course) and elected to bat.

Garthrigg How's experimental opening pair of gnarled, laconic Fred Padgett and smooth, bionic Richard Asquith built a foundation of 43 before the ancient left-hander missed one which, he said, swung a foot in the air before pitching on leg and hitting the top of off. After that, everybody else did their famous house of cards trick as five wickets went down for six runs. The glowing, sweating and glaring exception was Calum Cheyne, Garthrigg How's only Scottish fast bowler, who made a double-figure contribution and proved that he was in for his batting as well as his haircut, which makes Bobby Charlton look like King Charles the Second.

Murgatroyd had been obliged to make the journey wearing the Duck Hat, after last week's golden blob in the Scallion Cup, but he was able to transfer it quickly to another, who passed it on again, and a third time, and then back it came to Murgatroyd.

All four of these were adjudged LBW bowled Gorman, by an umpire — also called Gorman — who never for one moment allowed his father-son relationship with the bowler to influence his decisions.

With only 72 to bowl at, Cheyne cheered the visitors when he removed Oliphant first ball but there was no more reward to be had. High Hutton ground steadily on. First Asquith and then Walker made numerous inquiries regarding the symmetry of the LBW Law with events at the far end featuring the ball and different parts of Gorman's body.

However, the paternal umpire must have cleaned his glasses and turned up his hearing aid, as he had been advised to do by Garthrigg How players earlier in the afternoon, because he was now quite sure about such things as getting the finest of edges when playing back and smack in front to one which pitched well up on middle. This fine-edged batsman, Gorman, son of Gorman, was able to accumulate 32 out of 67 before an irate Walker stopped in his delivery stride and ran him out for backing up too far and too soon. The incident produced the usual friendly discussion in which players of both sides shared their ideas on sportsmanship, parentage and gentlemanly traditions, and Banks must have been swayed by the arguments because he put Murgatroyd on.

The script was put aside briefly as Murgatroyd, unable to decide if he was bowling seam-up or off-spin, took two wickets in his one over, but the long wait to opening time began immediately afterwards.

Garthrigg How 72, Padgett 21, Asquith 15, Cheyne 14. Gorman 4-21.
High Hutton 74-4, Gorman 32. Murgatroyd 2-7.
High Hutton 16pts, Garthrigg How 3pts.

(Editor's note: in the Nippon Missionary 4WD Fellside League, innings are 45 overs and points are awarded thus. Win—10; batting—one every 40 runs completed; bowling—one every two wickets. No draws. Tie—five points each)

Garthrigg How electrified

The silence was stunned in The Wintering Hogg on Sunday night after the visit of Swale Electricity in the first round of the Middleham Trophy. Garthrigg How had achieved the impossible!

They had improved on the previous day's collapse of five wickets for six runs. They lost six for five.

But we anticipate. With Naylor at first slip muttering non-stop about how difficult it was to get anyone to read his meter these days, Swale Electricity reached a low-key 128 off 40 overs.

Garthrigg How had started well when 41 for no wicket became 46 for 6 in no time at all, and the Man from Mars, Garthrigg How's only spectator, was kept busy retrieving far flung bats and pads for the next man in. He also lost no opportunity of telling anyone who would listen that this middle-order collapse meant that for two days running Dobber Metcalf had had a much shorter nap than he likes. But, he thought, this might yet prove a good thing in the end.

"You wait and see" said the Man from Mars. "There's always a happy cloud."

Smouldering with anger at the Electricity bowlers who thus curtailed his kip, Dobber smote 30 in boundaries, to no over-all avail.

First round losers do not go into a Middleham Plate but the Garthrigg How fixture secretary has apparently anticipated this and a full card is assured.

Swale Electricity 128-7, Hallgate 46.
Garthrigg How 96, Metcalf 30. Thorogood 3-13, Badger 3-29.

No headline for Garthrigg story

After a cricketless Saturday, with ex-Division 2 relegatees Nuncotes calling off in a thunderstorm, Garthrigg How ventured over the watershed into Westmorland on Sunday for a friendly match with (censored).

The pub in (censored) brews its own beer, the excellent quality and high strength of which was a novelty to the visitors and a proud credit to the home team.

The men of (censored) and your very own Garthrigg men are stout hearted and determined, with a powerful thirst for all that is just and good. Only Acts of God can render them incapable of cricket. Other perils, such as impact from aircraft and articles dropped therefrom, or snow, or raging blazes, are swept contemptuously aside when cricket requires.

What it was which prevented the aforementioned stout hearted men from disporting themselves on the greensward we shall never know.

Dobber Metcalf thought it was mass thrombosis. Wayne Satterdyke, school teacher, pointed out there was no such thing and it must have been mass lysteria.

In any case, readers of this column can be spared a report of what might have ensued, had egress occurred from the (censored) and (censored) Inn, (censored), in time for a 2.30pm start or, indeed, at all.

Gods have first laugh

The gods of cricket had some fun at Garthrigg How's expense on Saturday when they took up their positions in the sky over Fingby to watch Satterdyke and his men get as near as you can to a league win without actually bagging the 10 points.

Not that the situation ever looked terribly promising. When Asquith was out for 15 he had amassed half of the entire score at the time, which was a wholly unexciting 30 for 5 including seven extras. This cold, inanimate description of Garthrigg How's efforts encompassed the living Parks, Padgett and Donald 'Batman' Davies in his first match of the season, all failing to erode the sharp tip of the scorer's pencil.

The Duck Hat was moving around the pavilion like the collection plate in a Yorkshire synagogue. Later, the current Duckor, Davies, gave it to the fourth Duckee of the day, Metcalf, who was delighted in his turn to present it to Erickson for being similarly mindful of the high cost of graphite. Satterdyke and Halliday, however, were able to forget such cares and score a few.

In fact, Halliday beat his personal record by keeping out four straight ones in one innings which, against Fingby's bowling, gave him plenty of time in between to clout half a dozen boundaries and several others of the same intention. He and the watchful, wily Satterdyke were trundling along nicely at five an over, with Wayne getting one of them, when disaster struck.

The fifth and final straight one was eventually delivered by the stalwart Minter. Halliday returned to the pavilion in forlorn hope that Padgett might have left him a smoke in the packet, and in came Banks.

Garthrigg How were teetering on the verge of a second batting point and hopes were low, but Banks was too clever for Fingby.

He had on one old, blackened pad, one freshly Blanco'd, and of course his Cromagnon cream flannels which are the smoked-haddock colour of the ceiling at The Wintering Hogg. The work of art thus presented had Fingby transfixed, and Banks laid about him while he had the chance.

When Satterdyke was out, caught at mid-on for the 103rd time in his career, there was Cheyne, a Scottish fast bowler, to help Banks along. Banks and Cheyne always like a chat about this and that, which is what they were doing when Cheyne was run out by 15 yards.

The venerable wicket-keeper Cartmell views the quick single with a distaste appropriate to one of his long service, and Banks was soon back in the pavilion continuing his discussion with Cheyne on the theory and practice of running between the wickets. Ah well, 102 all out. Obviously not enough, without divine intervention.

After 20 overs, shared by Cheyne and Banks, Fingby were below par at 33 for 2. The wily Wayne called up Batman, he being the nearest thing to the supernatural option, and he caught and bowled top scorer Clark with his first ball. 10 overs later it was 69 for 6, and the next nine overs were bowled amid unbearable tension as Fingby scrimped and scraped to 101. Not that Batman noticed. He had the ninth wicket, caught with a tremendous dive and accompanying grunt by Cartmell, and was in the middle of telling the umpire the one about the lady vetenary surgeon and the guide dog when said official checked his pebbles and called "over".

101 for 9. One over left. It had to be a maiden, or a wicket maiden or, if you can have such a thing, a wicket part-maiden.

Satterdyke looked about him. There were many seasoned campaigners on the field, a number of them capable of bowling a devious last over in such a circumstance, but somehow they all seemed very busy, doing exercises or searching the blue yonder for enemy aircraft.

What could the skipper do? He put himself on and bowled a full toss from which they got two.

Garthrigg How 102, Halliday 37. Minter 4-27.
Fingby 103-9, Clark 21. Cheyne 3-37, Davies 4-18.
Fingby 17pts, Garthrigg How 6pts.

SUNDAY MAY 20

Garthrigg How have last laugh

On Sunday the gods of cricket were still laughing at Cheyne's 15-yard run out and Davies' joke about the vicar's daughter in the black pudding factory, and so they missed several remarkable sights.

The first was of both sides' pairs of opening batsmen walking out together at 2.30pm. The last came much later, when two Garthrigg How batsmen walked off the field having scored the winning runs.

Skipper Erickson was soon able to resolve the technical hitch which had caused the unusually bilateral start to the match. If the other skipper wanted to win the toss that much, well, let him.

Such deference by the Sunday leader is understandable when you realise that the friendly opposition at Garthrigg Hall that day was no less than Les Cigalles, from Harrogate. These are a nomadic team of youthful gentry named The Grasshoppers in French for reasons of their own, and they are not, as Dobber Metcalf thought, named after a famous Scarborough shitehawk called Leslie Seagull.

That Les Cigalles were at Garthrigg How was due to a phone call in mid winter from a desperate and unknown fixture secretary who had double booked and needed to get these insects off his hands.

Belinda the She-Dragon, Garthrigg How's fixture secretary, thought it might be nice to have some nice people in her nice pub for a change, and said yes.

Les Cigalles are stylish. They are the pride of their respectable families and late of our very best schools, with floppy hair cuts and high noses, and their openers take guard and gaze about the field as if expecting a round of applause for it.

If anyone deserved a round of applause it was the Man from Mars, standing in for five minutes as umpire while the regular official was trying to make his trouser zip work.

"I say, my dear old thing, is that two legs?" said the debonaire number one bat.

"No" said the Man from Mars.

The proper umpire ran out at this point, buttoning his white coat around him, and the Man from Mars returned to the boundary where he observed, while The Beast was marking out his run-up, that style isn't everything.

"These boys look pussy-fed to me" he remarked to himself.

"I think you mean spoon-footed" he replied.

Indeed, style and a sheltered upbringing were nothing against Walker at his most beastly, and before Garthrigg How's prize Richard went and sprained his ankle, the pitch, the light, the sightscreens and the government were being blamed in Les Cigalles' half of the changing hut for five clean bowled.

How to maintain the pressure? This was the thought uppermost in Erickson's mind and so he turned to Garthrigg How's leading admirer of public schoolboys, Barry Naylor.

Erickson said something to him about how he should forget his natural feelings of inferiority to these sons of gentlefolk. He should see their social position as irrelevant, and should concentrate instead on responding to a sporting challenge with his customary understated gusto.

Besides gusto, Erickson was also hoping that the French grasshoppers might be undone by Naylor's bowling action, and so it proved. All those many expensive, tutored hours in the school nets under the cynical eyes of walnut-skinned professionals, late of Yorkshire and Derbyshire CCCs, could give these fine young scions of purest Harrogate stock not the slightest premonition of what it is like to face Naylor in a good mood.

Seen from the batsman's point of view, Naylor looks like he's running towards you down the station platform as the train is leaving, waving an important item in his right hand which you, a passenger on the train, have forgotten. How could any grasshopper, much less a French one, expect such an action to result in an unbroken series of straight ones, on a length? One after another they fell, bemused.

They were unknown soldiers, the fallen. They probably had names like Herbert Fitzhilary and Hilary Fitzherbert but we shall never know since they brought no scorer and disdained to fill in the Garthrigg How book.

According to the scoreboard, numbers one to eleven managed 85 between them and then their opening bowler, number nine, showed how quickly it is possible for an adolescent member of the ruling class to bowl, and his 13 no-balls were second top scorer for Garthrigg How. Otherwise, their innings was remarkably straightforward and the Man from Mars walked back to his Reliant Robin flying saucer with a skip in his step.

Les Cigalles de Harrogate 85. Naylor 5-16.
Garthrigg How 89-3, Parks 24. No 11 3-34.

SATURDAY MAY 27

Memories not made of this

Lady Marjory's yew-tree topiary peacocks became shapeless, slanted, dark green ghosts as the wind howled across the grounds of Garthrigg Hall on Saturday, to greet the men of Gallinglath in the Nippon Missionary 4WD Fellside League Div 3.

Gallinglath is a wild spot, and the citizens thereof are clearly more used to playing cricket in a hurricane than our own lads. Indeed, massive Maurice Grindrod was so comprehensively at home in the storm that the Man from Mars was able to applaud a century. Otherwise the only sound above the wail of the gale was that of glass breaking in her Ladyship's walled garden as Grindrod hit two consecutive sixes, with the wind, off wits' end skipper Satterdyke.

Of Garthrigg How's attack, only Cheyne — a Scottish fast bowler — could remember his figures. Of our batsmen, only Satterdyke produced anything memorable as he continued his lifelong task of identifying, by trial and error, those opposition fielders who can hold a catch.

Gallinglath 173-5, Grindrod 101. Cheyne 2-23.
Garthrigg How 133-8, Satterdyke 42. Masham 4-50.
Gallinglath 18pts, Garthrigg How 5pts.

Batman nightflier in Garthrigg How victory

Few things are more satisfying to your very own Garthrigg boys than a win over Great Cubberthwaite. How pride and pleasure mingled after Sunday's knock-out win can be judged by the interesting fact that they made it to The Wintering Hogg a good two hours later than the norm, yet still managed to leave in the same condition as usual.

This match was ranked high in importance. As Batman said — "Mega wicked, Dobber. Unreal". As Dobber said — "Let's beat the ****s".

Nerves were further wracked as the start was delayed by an hour's heavy rain, but it was the Scallion Plate and so the roller was out as soon as the sun was, and excess water was squeezed from the pitch by repeated sideways ironing.

On this very difficult and unpredictable track, Parks and Asquith worked hard until a girl in Asquith's head took her jumper off and he was bowled. Erickson, up the order because some of the others hadn't arrived yet, would not be moved. When he was, the score had reached 61 for 2, but that wasn't what made the Man from Mars reach into his pouch for the last dry shreds of intergalactic black shag.

No, it was the manner of Macdonald's dismissal next ball which shocked all those present into uncontrollable fits. He claimed afterwards that he had been deceived by the bounce — the fourth bounce, that must have been — as he played two orthodox and two reverse sweeps at the same delivery. The ball had been slow and very short but even so had enough momentum to dislodge a bail after Macdonald came to the end of his impression of a demented metal detector.

The customary procession followed Macdonald and only Banks, 17, and Walker, 6 not out (beating last year's career-best innings by 20%), were able to give a good enough shove to the total.

It rained again at tea, causing more delay. Six overs after the re-start, Great Cubberthwaite were 2 runs for 3 wickets. Asquith and Walker were being exceptionally beastly, but Cubberthwaite skipper Bates remained adamant.

It was late, but not yet never. Erickson hated the thought of an unexpected victory reverting to an expected defeat as the score moved into the early 80s with eight overs left.

The moon came up to give a welcome sheen to the proceedings but there was no danger of an appeal against the light. It was the Scallion Plate, and in any case the umpires were giving everyone a glowing reference point by chain smoking.

It was dark. The enemy were getting close. An owl hooted. So, the answer had to be: Batman!

Donald Davies bowls at a military medium pace with no discern-able movement in the air or off the pitch. Naylor says Batman can both tell and bowl six jokes in an over, but even so, just occasionally . . .

The Man from Mars, peering at the cricket through his heat-seeking bifocals, remarked that he had seen Davies the previous night coming out of the Chinese take-away in Cronkley.

"He looked like his chips were down" he explained.

Batman's first ball was sent sizzling over the wall into the Marchion-ess's lettuces and beetroot, and Her Ladyship kindly lent a carbide-powered hurricane lamp to find it. The rest of Batman's over were all missed — probably the venerable keeper Cartmell was the only person who saw them — and then the moon went behind a cloud. Murga-troyd bowled Bates! Batman got another two! Not only that, but he brilliantly ran out the aptly named Darkling.

It was 94 for 9 and Batman to bowl. The equally aptly named Pratt played a huge hoik and sent up a skier into the twilight zone.

His team-mates' shouts of encouragement woke Banks from his poetic dreams and, as they politely drew his attention to the falling ball's position *vis-à-vis* his good self, he stuck out a hand and the ball stuck in.

Lady Marjory presented Pratt with his "I was caught by Barry Banks" T-shirt later in the pub, to wild acclaim, and Banks autographed it using the very same hand which had caught the ball which had given Garthrigg How victory over Great Cubberthwaite in the Scallion Plate, first round.

Garthrigg How 103, Padgett 21. Darkling 3-13.
Great Cubberthwaite 94. Murgatroyd 3-26, Davies 3-8.

Garthrigg How play Netherclough in the Scallion Plate 2nd Round on Sunday June 10th, at home.

SATURDAY JUNE 2 — RAIN

SUNDAY JUNE 3

Pram pushers roughed up

After the rain on Saturday had prevented all play at home to Sowerby Rudd in the League, Sunday's friendly visitors were those literary, artistic, well educated and modest fellows, the Perambulators, who were asked to bat first by Erickson, wielding as ever his personal King George VI tossing florin (1948).

The Man from Mars has remarked that Garthrigg men sometimes fail to be sufficiently wound up to the aggressive battle-peak required in strenuous League circumstances.

Likewise, we cannot always be sure that they will select for themselves the correct frame of unconcerned, unruffled, Sunday-friendly mind when confronted with a team of newspaper editors, bookwriters, estate agents, solicitors, architects and planning officers.

Such a preponderance of those operating in the housing market for a living caused the Man from Mars to exclaim:

"Woe unto them that join house to house til there be no place!"

Satterdyke assumed that this text from Isaiah, the Man from Mars' favourite book, was a call to arms. Erickson thought it was an aposite comment on the council's planning policy of village in-fill.

Naylor, not so much a biblical man as a devout Taurus, was flabbergasted to be asked to open the bowling and was even more so when his captain held three consecutive catches off his sidearm swingers.

Meanwhile the animous Asquith had been making the ball fly off a good length and the deeply muddled Perambulators, fending, pushing, hanging out washing or retreating to square leg, were soon five down for eight runs only.

A few moments later it was six out for 19, but cometh the hour and cometh Captain Clockstein, the author of a number of really interesting books on fossilised ferns. After shrugging off a blow over the heart from Asquith which would have felled many lesser and greater men, Clockstein settled in to put on 30 for the seventh wicket with budding defence lawyer Hart.

This trickle of runs, many of them in fact trickling between the hands of a tired and emotional Banks at squarish cover, was stopped by three daring measures of captaincy. The first was to place Naylor in one of Erickson's now annually traditional brand-new fielding positions. Barry N. was waved to a spot ten yards in front of the offender Barry B. and told he was fielding at Forward Short Banks.

The next item of strategy was to bring on the wily Wayne Satterdyke to bowl his deceptively flighted forward-and-back spinners.

So bemused were the batsmen by Satterdyke's run up — he bobs out from behind the umpire, then turns left in front of him, then turns right again to deliver the ball right arm over — that they were easy meat when the *coup de grâce* was administered by bringing on Walker.

The Beast had a problem getting his stump ball working, but once the direction finder was switched on the poor Perambulators could push only at the air while the lethal projectile fizzed past them on the way to keeper or off peg.

60 all out was hardly what the pram-pushers came for but Garthrigg How were pleased enough. They became progressively less pleased

as they struggled to 17 for 3 against bowling which caused the Man from Mars to say "That's more like it. Now, that's what you expect from people who've had central heating installed."

Jack Halliday went out to bat much moved by this speech. He put his first ball onto the roof of the Reliant Robin flying saucer and hit three fours off the other five balls he faced before receiving his nemesis, the straight one.

After that, Asquith had only to stick around with the patient Parks, still in from opening, to see the boys home.

Perambulators 60, Clockstein 16. Naylor 3-17, Asquith 2-7.
Garthrigg How 61-5, Parks 18 n.o, Halliday 18.

SATURDAY JUNE 9

Garthrigg How stiff, flabby and wide

Would your very own Garthrigg men achieve a Nippon Missionary 4WD Fellside League win as early in the season as the sixth Saturday? No, but in the process they proved a theorem: that which is stiff and hard at both ends can be soft and flabby in the middle, with a sting in the tail.

At home to the old enemy, Cronkley, a team which had won all its games this season and clearly expected not to be playing Garthrigg How next year, skipper Satterdyke lost the toss and was inserted.

Padgett was soon walking to the pavilion backwards, trailing his bat, having been adjudged in breach of the LBW Law, but Satterdyke and Parks got their heads down. This is usual in Parks' case but we can only assume that Satterdyke's head was heavy with guilt, at the remembrance of spending last evening drinking ten pints of Timothy Taylor's Landlord Bitter at The Wintering Hogg instead of watching The Cronkley Players do 'Waiting for Godot' in the Market Hall.

At 55 for 1, the Man from Mars observed that it was 3.15pm and coming up for harvest time, and sure enough batsmen began to return regularly to the pavilion complaining that the sun was in their eyes, the bounce was low, or Jamie Lee Curtis had come to them in a vision and promised a full night's entertainment if only Cronkley could win.

At 69 for 8 the venerable George Cartmell went out to bat, like a bank clerk going to work, and after watching a brief flurry from Cheyne must have felt a surge of responsibility as the Scottish fast bowler left the field, caught at deep mid wicket, to be replaced by Walker.

75 for 9. Well, old George might get 10, providing Walker was kept away from danger. It turned out that this wasn't Walker at all but rather some kind of three-dimensional hologrammic replica from the spirit world because he, or it, scored 29.

"The imposter" as the Man from Mars called him, very nearly quin-tupled Walker's previous career best in fine cavalier fashion, occasionally giving a cheery wave to a mysterious, short-skirted young lady on the boundary and — could this be true? — singing all the while.

Skipper Satterdyke thought the song might be "Til there was you", but Dobber Metcalf thought "My Ding-a-Ling" more likely.

With two runs wanted for a third batting point, Walker suddenly remembered he was the natural successor to Stewart Cammish, Gar-thrigg How's previous genuine number 11, and was bowled.

118. Not a great score, but never mind. Better than we thought at 69 for 8. Might just be enough.

These and similar phrases were uttered over tea in the snug sur-roundings of the She-Dragon's back bar, but Garthrigg How had reck-oned without the quality of Cronkley's batting.

The first two batsmen were warmly welcomed on to the field of play by their old Garthrigg pals, typifying the ancient cameraderie of cricket with their cheery greetings, forecasts of good fortune and constructive advice as regards suitable protective equipment for ten-der areas.

Unseduced, Hobson batted in splendid fashion. He managed to get himself out just short of his 50 but otherwise there was no trouble — until, at 115 for 1, a mid-pitch conversation took place between the two batsmen, or batswomen as Naylor kept insisting they were, just because they were called Darren Shirley and Kevin Bird. Apparently they were discussing ways of winning with 120 scored, rather than 119, so as to secure the extra batting point.

Erickson overheard the conversation, had a quiet word with Naylor, and then walked up to Asquith who was waiting at the end of his run. More words were exchanged. Deep fine leg was moved around to deep square. Before skipper Satterdyke could protest at this usurping of his authority, Asquith ran in with vigour and bowled a ball down the leg side so inaccurate that not even the venerable Cartmell could reach it. It went for four wides, and Cronkley were proud winners.

Garthrigg How 118, Parks 34, Walker 29. Shaw 5-20.
Cronkley 119-1, Hobson 48.
Cronkley 17pts, Garthrigg How 2pts.

SUNDAY JUNE 10

Scotch rocks in cup for Garthrigg How

The Scottish fast bowler is an infrequent Sunday player. Being the dutiful and slightly haggard bachelor that he is, he generally insists on the importance of having Sunday lunch with his old Mum, and since his old Mum always used to serve the beef and Yorkshire at 2.30pm when the pubs shut at two and still does the same, our Calum would be too late for cricket.

This Sunday was an exception, his old Mum's annual coach trip to Filey coinciding with a large party of ramblers from Bury St Edmunds booking in to The Wintering Hogg for lunch. Cheyne made himself available.

"Heroic" would not be too strong a word for his performance, starting with 17 overs, 5 maidens, 4 for 34 as Scallion Plate 2nd Round visitors Netherclough tumbled to 89 all out. This was a surprise to all, especially Netherclough who had been telling everyone in loud voic-

es that they were currently in fourth place in Division Two, no less, of the Nippon Missionary 4WD Fellside League.

The Netherclough debacle was ably assisted by a shortish, forty-something chap with a neatly trimmed beard who claimed to be Naylor despite wearing dazzlingly clean kit. Erickson had no hesitation in putting such a fine type of fellow on to bowl, and "Naylor" did indeed produce 22 overs, 10 maidens, 2 for 33 using a very creditable imitation of the authentic, pre-Alfred Mynn, Naylor action.

The Man from Mars said that watching Naylor, or "Naylor", bowl reminded him of his younger days when he used to go turkey catching at Christmas.

Passing for the moment over the excellent news that they have Christmas and turkeys on Mars, we must also mention Asquith.

Cheyne had been pounding in for 17 overs like a Shetland pony winning the Derby. He was ennervated. He needed relief. Asquith, inspired by his senior colleague's example, bowled six overs, 2 for 15. With two brilliant run-outs by Batman, one of which involved hitting the off stump on the full from the point boundary, Netherclough were bemused.

This fogginess of the intellect spread to Garthrigg How's batsmen as the two visiting opening bowlers, incredibly named Fox and Hunter, came walloping down like two wolves on the fold. For some reason they saved all their straight ones for whenever Halliday wasn't facing, and so it was that he got 34 while everyone else got, respectively, 9, 1, 4, 5, 6, 4, 7 and 4.

There is no need at this stage to assign particular names to those scores.

The crisis arrived. Halliday leaned on his carefree bat as the last but one partner came to the crease. It was Cheyne, and the score was 75 for 8.

The Man from Mars wondered if Calum Cheyne would get him some white pudding next time he went back to Cowdenbeath, and said he would ask him in a minute.

Eleven, yes, eleven agonising overs later, Cheyne was 12 not out, Halliday was 37 not out, and Garthrigg How had won, that's W-O-N, and were in the 3rd Round of a knock-out competition.

Netherclough 89. Cheyne 4-34, Asquith 2-15.
Garthrigg How 90-8, Halliday 37 n.o. Hunter 4-29.

Garthrigg How play Staggerthorpe Reserves in the 3rd Round of the Scallion Plate on Sunday June 25th, at home.

SATURDAY JUNE 17

Record books rewritten at Garthrigg How

160 off 45 overs could be considered a tolerably easy stroll up a low mountain, or you could think of it as just the right sort of challenge for a Saturday afternoon, or you could forget it altogether as totally impossible, depending on your psychology.

This week, away across the beck to local rivals Great Cubberthwaite in the Nippon Missionary 4WD Fellside League Div 3, the men of Garthrigg How amply demonstrated that no psychologist could ever fathom them as they switched by turns between all three points of view.

Saturday skipper Satterdyke won the toss and put the home team in, having seen Boycott on the television talking about greenness in the pitch at the Test Match. This greenness led Sir Geoffrey to expect the batsmen to struggle against fast bowling, by which he meant that after a morning session of 30 overs of cricket at the highest level, India might be 70 for 2.

The wicket at Great Cubberthwaite looked jolly green to Wayne, but then it almost always is and usually the home batsmen find the greenness to their liking and the boundaries within easy reach.

The Man from Mars, who comes to all away matches within five miles of Garthrigg Hall, ie this one and Cronkley, said "He shall feed me in a green pasture, and lead me forth beside the waters of comfort" — quoting from Psalms as a change from Isaiah.

Dobber Metcalf thought this meant that somebody might buy him a pint later in The Rough Lamb, but the Man from Mars was talking about cricket and he was in prophetic mode.

In went Great Cubberthwaite, anxious to redeem themselves after what they saw as a careless slip in the Scallion Plate, and skipper Bates did his usual imitation of a blinkered barnacle, holding the innings together while the rest all got a few. Nobody produced an outstanding performance but they all contributed — 12 here, 15 there, and it mounted up to 159 for 8.

Well, at least they didn't get a fourth batting point, which of course we will get when we win, won't we, said Batman at the interval. There was no response from the other tea-takers.

After tea, which was as expected — Great Cubberthwaite are league champions at making margarine and Shipham's paste go a long way — Parks and Halliday opened. The latter crashed his silk cuts with enormous power past unseeing fielders, and things were going well. At 47 for no wicket Halliday shouted "Banzai!" instead of "Wait!" and Parks returned to the pavilion muttering some less well known Japanese phrases.

Satterdyke went in and enjoyed himself while Halliday cut and pulled his way to 65 hearty runs. Then the Goddess of Straight Ones pointed her cruel finger and it was 107 for 2 with ten overs left.

Enter one Donald Davies, Batman to his friends, who had just finished telling the one about the three nuns going to confession and was going to start the one about the art mistress and the Aylesbury duck. Turning his mind for a moment to cricket, this fresh-faced 24-year-old teenager stopped telling jokes for three whole overs during which he smashed 25 runs and took Garthrigg How to 140 for 3.

What a strong position. 18 wanted off 42 balls with seven wickets left.

Bourne's "Empire" Cricket Scoring Book, Cumulative, now in its second century of publication, cannot have recorded many more dismal events than that which followed.

No sooner had Davies returned and got a quarter of the way through the one about the lighthouse keeper's week-end in Manchester, when a click was heard and a disappointed Satterdyke was surveying the bail-less stumps.

The next man spooned a slow full toss back to the bowler. Another swung wildly and played on and, as a queue formed at the dressing room pegs, a profound darkness gripped the soul of the Man from Mars.

"Woe unto them that rise up early in the morning that they may follow strong drink!" he declaimed, but no mere words, even those of his favourite prophet, could convey his feelings, and no further attempt was made.

He simply stood and watched as Garthrigg How lost six batspersons at, he calculated on his stellar navigational comptometer, an average of 0.83 (recurring) runs each, when the three who went in before them had averaged 40.3 recurring.

Great Cubberthwaite 159-8, Bates 37 n.o. Walker 3-30.
Garthrigg How 145, Halliday 65, Satterdyke 31, Davies 25.
Darkling 4-47, Pratt 3-52.
Great Cubberthwaite 18pts, Garthrigg How 7pts.

SUNDAY JUNE 18 — RAIN

SATURDAY JUNE 24

Power of the if-word in naval victory

Years ago, the wallers and dyke-diggers of Barrowmoor, that rural fastness beyond the charabanc's reach, would have considered themselves fortunate, privileged even, to tread the ancestral, nail-scissored cricketing turf of Garthrigg Hall. They, farm-yackers and apprentice blacksmiths all, would have been awed by the occasion.

Their defeat would have been a formality by such as the (relative) gentry of Garthrigg How, the Barrowmorians of yore being more used to playing cricket on whichever irregularly shaped and asymmetrically sloped bit of Barrow Common pasture could be scraped clean of sheep droppings for the afternoon.

Times have changed and, with the opening of their new sports centre, many fine cricketers of the officer class have rushed to join Barrowmoor CC, perhaps in the hope of catching a glimpse of the ladies' step-aerobics class coming out of the new sportsdrome.

Be that as it may, here they were at Garthrigg Hall and the days of burning your chickens are gone, said the Man from Mars. He was proved right as yet another Saturday League fixture demonstrated to Garthrigg How the enormous size of the word 'If'.

Richard Asquith has been feeling that it was time he wrested back the coveted 'Most Beastly' title from the other, younger and longer Dick, Walker, and today a rejuvenated Asquith escaped from his inhibitions and ran amok.

The faster Walker bowled, the more beastly Asquith became, and after 19 overs poor Barrowmoor were reeling at 36 for 5. Blood had been spilt, fingers had been split, and a broken tooth was found on the wicket. Never mind. Richard A's figures were 5 for 17.

The two openers had tried to play as per text book, but going forward down the line only resulted in spectacular catches at gully by Murgatroyd, catches of such heavier-than-air acrobatic qualities that no mother, not even his, could have seen them foreshadowed in the breakfast tea leaves.

Later Barrowmoor batsmen, seeing the ever lengthening run-ups of Asquith and Walker, plus the grin on Murgatroyd's face, preferred discretion to valour. Strong spirits wavered and powerfully built individuals were seen to quiver as they came to the wicket and took guard. How they retreated from the challenge! How they backed away to square leg, and fended and fenced!

Barrowmoor had that hunted look but eventually the beast in Asquith was satiated, and Walker's slim young body was over-extended, and so it was left to Banks, a much less brutal and less slim bowler, to remove their second half. This he did with his usual quiet and unassuming efficiency.

Some of the younger bowlers could learn from Banks. While they find it necessary to make clamour and shout while they dance, dervish-like, in appeal to the umpire, and then stare in strangled, anguished disbelief at the negative response, Banks finds a raised eyebrow sufficient question.

If the responsible official then says 'Not out!', well, a scratch of the nose-end and a hitch of the early Christian flannels says it all.

Even so, Banks had no immediate answer for a certain Commander Websdale, and while the other Barrowmorians progressed back and forth between wicket and pavilion, N R Websdale, 63, RN retd., scattered ducks and geese in the home-farm yard and disassembled Her Ladyship's runner bean wigwam with a six which cleared deep mid-wicket by 20 feet.

Eventually he missed the Banks straight one and that was that at 112; not a big target, surely.

If only Fred Padgett had been able to establish a lasting and meaningful relationship with any Garthrigg How batsman, such a total would have been easily reached. Instead he had to stand and shake his head in disbelief no less than five times as the seemingly innocuous off-spinners of Commander Websdale removed forward prodder after forward prodder, all bowled through the gate.

Padgett, being Fred and left handed, had to be different and was caught at slip. 78 for 6, which a brief flurry from Naylor turned into 97 for 9.

The venerable Cartmell and the vulnerable Walker then decided they would win it. 16 wanted off three overs. After the first of these, the Man from Mars observed that yet another quick single would see us taking a collection for the George Cartmell Memorial Fund, but the second over consisted of five dot balls and a four which zipped off George's top edge over third man, who had crept in too short in his eagerness.

While Barrowmoor's captain explained the basic tenets of fielding positions to the unfortunate enthusiast, Cartmell and Walker discussed how they were going to get seven off the last over. No clear plan emerged.

The visiting skipper took the ball. Cartmell square cut the first with D'Artagnan-like delicacy, and if only there had not been an outstretched boot he would have got four instead of one. Six wanted. Walker played a stroke, reminiscent of Fred Astaire and silver-topped cane, which resulted in two to deep square.

Mindful of his partner's low-voltage pacemaker, Walker took plenty of time arranging himself for the next ball which, despite a wind-whistling flourish of the bat, landed safely in the keeper's gloves.

Three balls left. Four runs wanted. Walker hit the next one with a part of the bat not normally facing frontwards and the resulting skier was watched by all in paralysed fascination. In fact, Cartmell had time to run up to Walker's end and if only he had been able to attract the boy's attention things might have been different. As it was, he had to go all the way back again, just as the fielder, the same who was late of too-short third man, spilled the returning ball onto the ground. Commander Websdale suggested to the Barrowmoor skipper that the proposed disembowelling of the fielder in question would be better done at home rather than on the Marchioness' field, and so the last ball was delivered.

It was a short, slow grubber. Walker hit it off the tee, as it were, and topped it. It went to mid off for one.

Barrowmoor 112, Websdale 31. Asquith 5-34, Banks 5-42.
Garthrigg How 110-9, Padgett 47. Websdale 6-32.
Barrowmoor 16pts, Garthrigg How 7pts.

SUNDAY JUNE 25

Milk Marketers cancelled owing to Scallion Plate

Small earthquake at Staggerthorpe. Not many there

Garthrigg How went away in the Scallion Plate 3rd round on Sunday, to Staggerthorpe, fully expecting to return with their crests fallen. The opposition was Staggerthorpe Reserves and, of course, it is common practice to make favourable adjustments downwards with your first teamers into the alleged Reserves when there is a pot in sight.

Staggerthorpe 1st XI play in the Two Counties Alliance, indeed, and the unstrengthened Reserves a division above Garthrigg How in the Nippon Missionary 4WD Fellside League, so what hope was there? Ah but, it so happened that this Sunday the Minor Counties had a match with the Indian touring side, and called up three from the Two Counties Alliance Combined XI who were therefore short for their game against MCC Under 18s.

Three Staggerthorpe first teamers were thus needed versus the yellow and red juniors, leaving Staggerthorpe short for their VAT 69 Village Vase tie with far-away Harleston in Norfolk, so three leading lights of the Reserves had to go, or 'goo' as they say down there in Harleston.

Dennis Palfreman was organising the annual Staggerthorpe Steam Rally, which meant he and two other 2nd XI regulars were unavailable, and the consequence was that the said Reserves turned up for the Scallion Plate with their seven least desirable men, plus two 12 year olds.

Staggerthorpe Reserves 16, Phelps (aged 12) 6. Asquith 5-5, Walker 5-8.

Garthrigg How 17-0.

Garthrigg How play Little Battisford in the Scallion Plate semi-final on Sunday July 15, away.

Hawkers floored by flying pigs

Several airborne Gloucester Old Spots were spied in the moonlight on Friday night, a portent for the following day's cricket.

So it proved as the sun shone over Crosby Hawker, second in the 3rd Division of the Nippon Missionary 4WD Fellside League. Little did they know that, at their backs, the time of their doom was hurrying ever nearer in Cecil Hardwick's winged chariot minibus, part exchange welcomed.

An inspired performance by Barry Banks, he of the pre-Cambrian britches, bowling 16 overs for only 19 runs, was chiefly responsible for keeping Crosby to a score low enough for Garthrigg How to think about getting.

Metcalf's interlude attempts to read the bones of fortune — in this case, bones retrieved from a sardine sandwich and dropped into skipper Satterdyke's tea — could cast no light on the likelihood of Garthrigg How being able to amass 91. No assistance from the fifth dimension proved necessary as Padgett and Asquith were quite determined. They collected singles and twos, took no chances, and by the time Harrison had bowled both of them the victory platform looked secure, needing only a few more planks and a coat of paint.

In came Halliday, in whose hands a four and a half inch piece of willow can sometimes assume the dimensions of a plank, and whose innings often make his skipper think he would rather be walking one. But this was a Halliday day and after some mighty blows from the heart of oak, followed inevitably by a vain wave at a straight one, Garthrigg How were 77 for 4.

Skipper Satterdyke went in muttering about losing from better positions than this, but he and Naylor chipped away and, what do you know, Garthrigg How won a league match!

Crosby Hawker 90. Banks 3-19, Walker 3-39.
Garthrigg How 91-4, Harrison 4-30.
Garthrigg How 17pts, Crosby Hawker 4pts.

Piggles flies again !

Yes, amazing to relate, Squadron Leader Pigglesworth's 'Red Pigs' display team performed on two consecutive days in Garthrigg How CC's airspace, and their precision flying was identical on each day with the tiniest of variations.

The visitors to Garthrigg Hall were the soaraway lads of Sunbiggin, a team which Garthrigg How have watched zoom by them in the league, from Division 4 to Division 2 in consecutive seasons. Meanwhile the antediluvian mid-season friendly has been maintained with its traditionally amicable but competitive spirit.

This match was more closely contested than any league game, and Sunbiggin must have been surprised to be inserted after losing the toss. Skipper Erickson was confident, however, that a new tactic of keeping beastliness to one end while offering gift vouchers at the other would be Sunbiggin's downfall.

Indeed the snorting Walker, having been told by Erickson that he was on a promise with the new French *assistante* at Cronkley Grammar should he take five wickets, has never bowled better.

His accuracy and fearsome pace were perfectly mirrored by Banks at the other end, with ten overs of gentle rubbish so varied in direction and trajectory that Sunbiggin's men were totally flummoxed.

Erickson then wrought a double bowling change, guaranteeing four-wicket Walker another spell later, and put Asquith and Satterdyke on. This was too much for Sunbiggin who completely shut up shop, so that after two hours' play they were 80 for 8 and not in favour of Sunday opening.

Back came Walker, his heart beating wildly at the thought of the pretty madamoiselle, but it was the deeply unsporting Satterdyke who wrapped up the business with his wily combination of double-looped top, back and side-to-side spin.

After tea, Padgett and Parks put together a solid opening. They were slow, but from an hour of hard graft there were 39 runs on the telegraph and some cause for the Man from Mars to speculate that this might turn out to be Garthrigg How's third consecutive victory.

"Look before you slip", he said mysteriously, and Fred Padgett was immediately adjudged out, LBW.

Showing his unqualified agreement with the umpire in the usual way, Fred complimented the said official, as he went past him, walking slowly and backwards the better to enjoy social intercourse, on his excellent eyesight, sporting acumen, sparkling intellect and detailed intimacy with the Laws of Cricket. The umpire gave Fred a cheery wave with a limited number of fingers and Satterdyke went in to bat.

It immediately became apparent that wily Wayne had not yet completed his long-term study of the catching abilities of North Riding mid-ons, and so it was left to others to continue with the main task of the day. Two more quick wickets fell before Naylor steadied the tottering tower and climbed grindingly upwards.

The overs were nearly gone and eleven runs were wanted when Metcalf and Erickson were woken from their slumbers by the sound of falling timber.

While the Man from Mars created a diversion by running onto the field with drinks, one at once, Metcalf was able to don his fighting gear and get out there before anyone noticed that two minutes had elapsed a number of times. Erickson too was ready as Metcalf ran Parks out, perhaps taking previous offences into consideration, and suddenly it was all at boiling point.

Noting that ten were wanted off nine balls, Metcalf and Erickson decided to get them in singles and were thus able to keep the cheering crowd on their toes until the very last ball of the day.

Sunbiggin 90. Walker 4-21, Satterdyke 3-22.
Garthrigg How 91-6, Asquith 24.

Part Three

THE SEASON, SECOND HALF

T-shirt sales soar while Garthrigg How collapse

This week's visiting muggers from the Nippon Missionary 4WD Fellside League Division 3 were Nuncotes, relegated from Division Two last year and so largely unknown to the home side since the away game was rained off earlier in the season.

Garthrigg How expected hard going, and got it, although as Walker and Asquith were both missing from the attack things might have been much worse.

No, they couldn't have been very much worse, but Nuncotes had to bat out their 45 overs before Garthrigg How could prove once again that they never can miss an opportunity of surpassing themselves.

The Scottish fast bowler Cheyne put in his usual high quality performance and with Banks also being niggardly, after 25 overs Nuncotes were the club bores with 65 for no wicket. Saturday skipper Satterdyke, seeing that Banks was not so young as he was when he began his bowling spell, turned for inspiration to Naylor.

Barry Naylor, fearing to re-open an old ear wound, likes to keep his bowling arm well away from the side of his head. None of the Nuncotes men was alive in the round-arm days and so they'd never seen anything like it.

Naylor, crafty as ever, softened them up with three wides then got the top man Bunwell out, caught by T-shirt merchant Banks (*see below). Others fell gradually to what Nuncotes must have felt was a surprisingly modest total, some of them to a surprisingly modest

Satterdyke who bowled 10 overs for only 41 runs, taking four wickets the while with his break-back triple floaters.

Indeed, 132 off 45 overs is not a great score. Mr Arthur Scargill (no relation) is not a bowler of high repute — rarely, even by his own admission, worthy of any more sparkling an accolade than "can be naggingly accurate".

However, as the Man from Mars observed, constipation counts for nowt in the grounds of Garthrigg Hall, and records are made to be played.

Indeed they are, and Mr Arthur Scargill was about to become famous. Banks, Erickson, Murgatroyd and Halliday were among those batsmen who spent more time on their journey than at their destination, as Scargill and his colleague White enjoyed two purple patches.

In one of these, Garthrigg How scored four singles and lost four wickets. In the other, they scored no singles and lost four wickets.

Nuncotes 132-9, Bunwell 34, White 29. Satterdyke 4-41, Naylor 3-20. Garthrigg How 42, Padgett 17. Scargill 6-10, White 3-13. Nuncotes 18pts, Garthrigg How 5pts.

*T-shirts for Nippon Missionary 4WD Fellside League batsmen bearing the legend "I've been dropped by Barry Banks" are available at all good and bad stores. The much rarer, hand-printed shirt, with "I've been caught by Barry Banks", can be had free on application, if accompanied by two signed witness statements and a copy of the scorebook, from Mrs Smailes, The Wintering Hogg Inn, Garthrigg How.

SUNDAY JULY 15

Parks in equilibrium

Few reasons can there be for cancelling the annual trip to far-away Seamer, near Scarborough, where the cricket is always followed by outstanding hospitality, a sumptuous dinner at The White Horse (as Fred insists it is still called) and a search for stragglers at chucking-out time in forgotten corners of the Mayfield and the Londesborough Arms.

But there is one reason. Being in the semi-final of the Scallion Plate against Little Battisford.

Little Battisford, a small village rather like Horsehouse in Coverdale except with fewer palm trees, is a magic place of fear and dread where the wicked whisker of worse luck can flicker and twitch more than Fred Padgett's left eyebrow when forced into a round-buying situation.

The ground is about the smallest anywhere, and yet big scores are rarely made because the wicket is so sporting. Armour plated cod pieces and chain-mail buttock pads are required against all bowling above the very slowest in pace, and many are the fallen wickets resulting from an over-confident swipe towards the near-by boundary.

Garthrigg How batted first and immediately lost Asquith and Padgett. Murgatroyd and Satterdyke fiddled and puddled along, then the skipper popped one up towards mid on, shouted "Mine!" and went for the run.

Murgatroyd, with feudal loyalty, allowed himself to be run out, and in came Parks.

Since the new opening partnership of Asquith and Padgett was formed, Parks has pined. His runs have been few, his brow furrowed. He has worn a gloomy mein, as if dark thoughts were at work deep inside his animus. Now, at last, he was to enjoy his demotion to No 5 with a faultless and stylish top score in his team's total of 114.

As the weather turned cold, the clouds gathered, the Battisford Banshee began to howl aback of Fountains Fell and the Head Troll of Ingleborough cast the boiled cat's bones, so did the Fates decree that 31 was today's number of destiny, for Parks and for Little Battisford alike.

With Walker at one end frightening them to death and Naylor at the other being naggingly accurate, the poor lads of Battisford never had a light.

The two left handers went to Naylor, one man was run out, and Walker did the rest including six clean bowled with a hat-trick.

The last was caught in the slips by Parks, and in all the excitement nobody at the time noticed the perfect similarity between two totals, one amassed by an individual and one by eleven.

Garthrigg How 114, Parks 31 n.o. Allen 3-14, Bates 3-34.
Little Battisford 31. Walker 7-17.

Garthrigg How play Cronkley in the final of the Scallion Plate, at Great Cubberthwaite on August 12.

SATURDAY JULY 21

Some heroes do it again

For various reasons, including hay-timing, mis-timing and two-timing, the team to face Fingby at home in the Nippon Missionary 4WD Fellside League was not constituted in the same way as that heroic band of last week's Scallion Plate semi-final.

The winning streak continued even so, and one begins to wonder what feats there could be beyond the abilities of Garthrigg How CC.

While admitting that last week's great win was welcome as the showers in May, the Man from Mars added even more graphically that it was a storm on a molehill — but Garthrigg How's pragmatic and only spectator is not always right.

Youthful exuberance showed the way as the Beastly Boy, Walker, removed Clark and Wallis, Fingby's leading scorers, at a personal cost of 8. The visitors then took control and it needed a sudden burst from Asquith to redress matters. He had been dreaming on the long-on boundary about the second-hand value of engagement rings when skipper Satterdyke promised a lend of his *Penthouse* magazine if he took a wicket.

The Scottish fast bowler also got in on the act, having been promised a lend of Satterdyke's book about hair transplants, and Fingby were lurching on 119 for 6.

Some defiant tail-wagging and generous fielding allowed a bigger total than had been foretold, but a highly impressive opening partnership between Padgett and Asquith put Garthrigg How back on top. The saturnine veteran, last season's OP of the Y, hit eight 4s in his 44 while his dashing young colleague picked off the ones and twos and kept him on his mettle.

Their departure, on either side of Naylor — plumb LBW for the first time in his life — caused flutters of concern, but Batman's nonchalance, not to mention his two huge sixes off Minter into Lady Marjory's ridge cucumbers, showed that this was to be Garthrigg How's day.

When Davies went, confidence was so brimming that Murgatroyd and Cheyne had no trouble doing the necessary.

Fingby 164-9, Newman 40, Deveraux 29. Walker 5-64.
Garthrigg How 165-5, Padgett 44, Davies 38, Asquith 31. Minter 4-46.
Garthrigg How 18pts, Fingby 6pts.

SUNDAY JULY 22

Bee sting, and carrots by moonlight

Buttle is a tiny village, a hamlet really, of a few houses, two farms and a pub, over the hills and far away, and yet they always have managed to produce a good cricket team. Garthrigg How's annual visit to Buttle is looked on both as a severe test for Cecil Hardwick's recycled minibus and as a chance to visit a part of the North Riding where they get frosts in July, but never is the cricket to be seen as a mere rural thrash. Buttle may only play Sunday friendlies, but they are no walk-over for the relatively cosmopolitan big-league guys from down below.

Buttle began slowly in warm sunshine against the assertive pair of beasts, Asquith and Walker, and for ten overs nothing much happened.

There is an upright sheet of corrugated iron in the Buttle sportsfield which has GENTS painted on it, also I LOVE MARGARET LOFT-

HOUSE. It is at deep third man or deep mid-on next over, and Fred Padgett, Garthrigg How's lugubrious wiseacre who doesn't like fielding in the deep, had stood in front of it without moving for all of those ten overs.

Suddenly he became animated, waving his arms and jumping about. Sunday captain Erickson thought that perhaps he wanted a bowl and went over to tell him that his left-arm lobs would not be required just yet, only to learn that a bee had stung him on the inside of his right nostril.

Fred went off to seek medical aid, no easy matter in Buttle on a Sunday afternoon, and the batsmen now began piercing the diluted field with style and regularity. Young Drayton looked to be a very promising player and was especially at ease against Banks, AKA the ragged trousered philanthropist, who was giving the ball his usual early swing and Drayton many generous opportunities for profit.

Just about everybody had a bowl except Padgett, returned after having vinegar put up his nose by Mrs Bousfield, Stony Haggs Farm. Although wickets fell no-one was able to stop the run feast. Meanwhile a large black cloud had appeared from behind the fell, obscuring the sun and threatening to spoil the match.

In the event, it released its most ungentle rain all through the tea interval and for half an hour afterwards, then the sun came out and steam began rising from the wicket.

Garthrigg How were set to get 166 on a soaked surface, a task which was made to look increasingly unlikely by Buttle's hostile bowling. Asquith had gone forward to his first ball from Sloper and got a very close view of the maker's name as it passed the end of his nose. After that, Garthrigg players preferred to lean back, bats dangling, in the belief that cricket was a good game but not worth dying for.

At 19 for 4 Murgatroyd strode forth, five foot three in every direction, a mobile ziggurat of sweaters and pads beneath a shadowing cap which concealed a firm jaw and a determined lip. He joined Erickson and after a few alarums this pair dug in. When they felt they were well dug, they began to lay about them and a surprising quantity of success rewarded their efforts.

The black cloud came back but, amid the encircling gloom, hope shone as two of the less outstanding examples of Garthrigg How big hitters scored fours and sixes and generally took apart the previously fearsome attack.

Alas, the gloom became too encircling for Erickson, who often has difficulty seeing the ball even in good light, and the visitors were 83 for 5 off 27 overs with another 13 to go. In marched Dobber Metcalf and, without bothering to take guard or consult his partner, hit his first three balls for four.

They carried on in the same chirpy mood and, on the brink of victory, with just seven wanted, Metcalf pulled a long hop high and far in the direction of mid wicket. They ran three, but none counted, for news was brought from beyond that Dobber had been held by whoever was fielding over there.

This, obviously, was a man reared on raw carrots, or possibly large quantities of red palm oil and watercress which are also plentiful of Vitamin A.

His night vision would have done credit to the owls which were by then perching along the top of the sightscreen, waiting for the cricket to finish so that the mice might come out from under the pavilion — a fine example, incidentally, of early 20th century coachwork, once the property of the South Durham & Lancashire Union Railway and still with its original curtains.

It was almost 9pm. How distant now seemed the sunlit, bee-sting period when, one argument went, the Buttle batters had been able to see the ball to hit it and, the other argument went, the fielders had been able to see to stop it.

The moon came out, that silver beacon in whose beams all things have been seen and noted, and the venerable Cartmell came out, that silver bacon saver who has seen everything but not done all of it. But would he do it tonight?

Cartmell is a master of the nudge, the tickle and the late prod. No-one still alive has ever seen him play a drive, or indeed a front-foot shot of any kind.

He nurdled one off the last ball of the over, and mardled another off the first of the next. Murgatroyd swished in violent optimism at a piece of the air which seemed darker and more solid than the rest, and somehow connected with the fifth. The ball went, but they knew not where and the umpires agreed that four had been scored. A single was scrambled off the last ball. Garthrigg How, far from home, and especially Murgatroyd, but a flickering shade in the gloaming, had earned their Victory Ale.

Buttle 165-8, Drayton 44, Boothby 29 n.o.
Garthrigg How 166-6, Murgatroyd 54 n.o, Erickson 40, Metcalf 40. Sloper 3-40.

SATURDAY JULY 28 — RAIN

SUNDAY JULY 29

Star twinkles, Padgett winkles, Erickson tinkles

The rain which was forecast for the week-end arrived on time and made Saturday's League journey to Gallinglath unnecessary, but the clouds parted over Cronkleydale on Sunday for the home game with the occasional nomads of the Fellside Young Farmers. This annual mismatch provided its unfailingly regular supply of cricketing incidents, using the term 'cricketing' in its widest sense and mismatching the teams in the opposite direction from what you might expect. Sunday leader Erickson's first shock came when he noticed that, among the standard collection of short-haired, open-faced, brawny youths in jeans, check shirts and trainers, stood an altogether more elegant figure sporting a track suit which would have taken a month to pay for at the NFU minimum wage rate.

That this unorthodox cricket wear was a concession to his non-white team-mates rather than his usual playing apparel, became obvious when he placed his own bat, his own pads and his own gloves all ready on top of his very capacious designer kit-bag.

"You know who that is, don't you" stated the Man from Mars to the puzzled Erickson outside the changing hut. "It's Morrison" he continued, without waiting for an answer. "Played for the Minor Counties last week against Combined Universities."

Of course. The said Morrison was the regular wicket-keeper with Northumberland. He played his club cricket for Morpeth and lived up there, but his father still had the farm at Crabstack, above Cronkley, which doubtless accounted for his selection today.

"It's a good job George watered the wicket, then, isn't it?" said Erickson as he fingered his King George VI tossing florin (1948) in his trouser pocket.

A few minutes later the YF skipper called heads, it came down tails, and Garthrigg How's men, correctly attired except for Banks, took the field.

Asquith's first ball went for six. His second went straight up into the ionosphere and by the time it fell into the horny hands of Fred Padgett the batting boys had gawped, galloped up and down a bit, and eventually crossed.

In came the tall, cultured figure of Morrison, his Northumberland cap in classically formal position, his track suit irridescent in the sunlight, his pads, made of the latest space-shuttle materials, immaculate. While Erickson talked earnestly with Asquith, an almost indiscernable smile of confidence, perhaps even of disdain, accompanied Morrison's look of serene concentration as he settled into his stance.

Just as Asquith began his run up, Erickson called him to stop. Apologising most sincerely to Morrison, the captain made two minor adjustments to the field, sending mid-on and mid-off back another ten.

Asquith ran in again. Almost before he had let go of the ball, Morrison was moving onto the front foot looking for an educated push for one to get him off the mark.

The ball pitched just short of a length, reared up and zipped past the end of Morrison's rapidly withdrawing nose with a ferocity worthy of Sir Frederick Sewards Trueman. The slap of it hitting George Cartmell's gloves could be heard all over the dale, as indeed could the chortling of Naylor at first slip.

The next three balls were almost identical, the only variation being the precise distance in millimetres between the retreating proboscis of Morrison and the fizzing missiles being bounced off a non-first-class pitch by Asquith.

This contest, between the extra beastly Richard and the imperturbable Morrison of superior mein, was not resolved. Morrison was there at tea, with 15 not out, all in singles, and Asquith's vengeance had had to be taken on other, more bucolic victims, including Son of Fred Padgett, bowled for a golden blob.

76 for 6 didn't seem much of a score and it was no real surprise when the Young Farmers took up the unusual option of batting on after the Ty-Phoo and sandwich spread.

While Morrison continued to bear himself like the star he undoubtedly was in spheres other than this, meanwhile adding two more singles to his score, a huge lad came in whom Erickson recognised as Hector Pithey, this year's hay-bale tossing champion at Garthrigg How fete. Presumably finding a bat just as easy to wield as a pitchfork but the ball much more projectable than a bale of hay, Pithey hit 28 off five balls of a rare Erickson over, before being bowled by the sixth.

Padgett and Asquith opened the innings for Garthrigg How with 45 minutes to six o'clock, plus 20 overs, to get the runs. Erickson, risking his life by pinching a fag out of Padgett's packet, groaned when he saw the ball was being tossed to Son of Fred.

Padgett Senior would never allow himself to be out to his offspring and so extreme caution would be applied. Son bowled three consecutive maidens to father while Asquith took a two at the other end, then there was a single. Son of Fred to Asquith.

The young man's action, modelled on his father's left-arm backhand grenade tosser, gave the ball a tremendous amount of air and no pace. Asquith, undecided between a six over midwicket, a leg glance and a square cut, produced a forward dither and lost his off bail.

There was more of this, and more, and Erickson's groans were loud and long by the time the score was 27 for 8 with 13 overs to go.

In went the skipper to join Father Padgett, still there on a gallant and gritty 5. Erickson winked to the old boy and took an elaborate time over his guard and field-placing survey, having previously noticed a large, black and threatening cloud heading directly for Garthrigg Hall.

As Son of Fred began his five pace jog-up, Erickson raised a hand apologetically and complained about a drop of sweat getting onto his glasses. Taking off the batting gloves, and then the spectacles, and getting out the large red and white spotted kerchief all took up a few moments, but the real gem was the special little shake he gave to his specs, causing the left lens to fall out onto the grass.

Of course the lens was retrieved immediately but the tiny screw which holds the frame together took some finding, as did a screwdriver fine enough to screw it. The absent-minded Erickson forgot to mention the small silver penknife which he had kept in his trouser pocket for this purpose ever since he sat on his glasses during an embarrassing moment after one of Lady Marjory's parties.

If one of the Young Farmers had not thought of the Garthrigg How first aid kit, in which there happened to be a scalpel, they might have been seeking a screwdriver yet.

Such agricultural presence of mind went unrewarded, because raindrops fell as the players resumed their positions and a torrential downpour ensued, making the draw as certain as immediate adjournment to The Wintering Hogg was practical.

Fellside Young Farmers 111, Pithey 28. Asquith 5-50.
Garthrigg How 27-8. Padgett 6-12.

Birthday present almost arrives

A flustered Garthrigg How CC piled into Cecil Hardwick's converted minibus, available for hire except W.I. outings, on Saturday, en route to Sowerby Rudd, with no less than five non-standard irregular persons, one of whom had only come along to score.

This state of affairs was due to a sudden outbreak of She-Dragon's Chorea, which is something like motor neurone but temporary, consequent upon a Friday pre-birthday celebration hosted by a well known local school teacher and cricket captain. Also, two senior players had made religious objections, remembering what happened to them the last time they went to Sowerby Rudd.

Last minute replacements are always difficult to deal with, thought pro-tem skipper Erickson. Do you thank them for turning out by batting them high up the order and giving them a bowl, or do you remember why they weren't picked in the first place and have them in for their fielding?

When he saw the pitch, which looked like it had been imported from the top of Great Whernside, Erickson decided the newcomers could not be risked against fresh bowlers and so Padgett and Asquith began and put on 30. Wickets seemed to fall with much more space between them than usual and the Garthrigg How cheap return at party rate did not occur.

Jack Halliday tuned up his biceps for next week's Transpennine Tup Throwing championships and laid about him mightily, disturbing many forms of wildlife. Indeed, Halliday raised a cheer from both sides when his six into the next field produced startled cries from a mating pair of Leatherjackets. Whether they came back later to complete their conjunction, or indeed to retrieve their crash helmets, we shall never know.

When Halliday finally got his fatal straight one, it was the turn of the first Garthrigg How new boy, a self-confident trainee hammock-tester by the name of O'Kane. He missed the ball eight times, hit it four times for 18 runs, then missed it again.

Now we had regular reserve Macdonald, top man at Garthrigg How County Primary, who had been told by Padgett that League rules were different. In the League you had to get it over the cricket-field boundary without bouncing for four, and the parish boundary for six. This rule seemed OK by Macdonald.

Meanwhile Banks, who has recently had his flannels valued at Sotheby's, was spreading panic among opposition and associates alike, tempting all three Fates at once, establishing new standards in brink-manship and exploring the farthest limits of the umpiring principle of the benefit of the doubt.

No matter what he did, however, he could not be out that day nor, later, could he find anyone who knew what was meant by "Dephlogis-ticate", which he was fairly sure was what the Sowerby Rudd lads had said he should go and do with himself.

Lucky and carefree Garthrigg How reached 157, hurtfully close to a fourth batting point but excellent nevertheless, and at first it looked like it would prove plenty.

With Banks and Asquith firing them in, and astonishing catches from O'Kane and Macdonald, Sowerby Rudd were staggering on 24 for 2 off 11. Little did we know that our out-of-sight skipper was not the only birthday boy. Sowerby Rudd's anniversarian was called Keswick, and he had all 18 of his birthdays, plus most of his Christmases and Chinese New Years, all in the space of 45 minutes. When at last his Yom Kippur arrived, in the shape of the famous Asquith unplayable leg-stump yorker (if only he knew how he did it), it was too late. The tide had swung, as the Man from Mars might have said.

Home skipper Bacher had opened the batting and clearly meant to be there ready for next week, and with bowling resources thin there was little to be done. Grindingly, certainly, and despite enormous spirit from the ever-optimistic fielders, another Garthrigg How defeat arrived on time.

Perhaps that question Erickson asked himself, about why the ir-regulars were not picked in the first place, should be asked again.

Garthrigg How 157, Halliday 38, Macdonald 32, Banks 21.
Sowerby Rudd 160-3, Keswick 73, Bacher 61 n.o.
Sowerby Rudd 19pts, Garthrigg How 4pts.

SUNDAY AUGUST 5

Advert proves prophetic

In the early days of commercial television, when you wondered where the yellow went, the Esso sign meant happy motoring, graded grains made finer flour and 1001 cleaned a big, big carpet for less than half a crown, viewers were frequently told that a Double Diamond worked wonders.

"A Double Diamond works wonders, so drink one today" we were tunefully advised in those happy times when consumers were understood to have common sense and to be in no need of protection against light-hearted advertising claims.

Of course, some people may have taken the advice further, on the assumption that if one Double Diamond worked wonders, two would work miracles, three would bring about the Second Coming and four would see Darlington win the FA Cup.

Most of the public did realise that increasing numbers of Double Diamonds would eventually produce an equal and opposite effect to wondrousness and may even result in paralysis, mesmerism and horizontality.

Consider, therefore, the plight of Sunday skipper Erickson when, knowing that his team for the day was a haphazard collection of asymmetrical occasionals, he received a certain Clunk Metcalf, cousin of Dobber, into the changing hut at 2.29pm.

Clunk got married the previous week and had still not fully incor-porated the experience.

"Match starts at 2.30" said the skipper.

"Shorry am late. Held pardon helduperic. Diffcul. Shorry."

"Get your pads on. You're opening with me" said the affirmative Erickson, and turned away.

"Woh?" said Clunk.

Eight overs later the Garthrigg How score was 65 for no wicket, of which Erickson had scored the 5.

Clunk Metcalf, carrying within his person the equivalent in premium lager of at least 20 Double Diamonds, was working such wonders that poor Ravenstone, visitors for the day, could do nothing but spread their field far and wide and await the inevitable mistake.

It was not long in coming. In the 12th over, with his personal score on 89 and the team total on 97 for no wicket, Metcalf gave a huge hoik across the line, missed, and was hit on his recently solemnised parts.

He went down as if humanely killed and had to be taken away. Later, he accused Erickson of hurrying him in the changing hut so that he forgot to put his box on.

Meanwhile, Garthrigg How staged a connoisseur's example of a middle-order collapse and were all out for a very disappointing total. With only ten men they could not stop Ravenstone from producing a second half of the match which was as boring as the first had been exciting.

Garthrigg How 128, Metcalf 89 retired dead, Erickson 13 n.o.
Ravenstone 130 for 7, Collingwood 48 n.o.

SATURDAY AUGUST 11

Triangle excited

The shivering and quivering of aroused spirits was visible in the air of the North Dales Triangle as dawn broke on the first day of the most important week-end in cricketing history.

This was a day, August 11th, noted as the anniversary of the 1953 earthquakes in the Ionian Islands. Here in the North Riding, many leagues from our Grecian friends, the date was surely going to live up to its international reputation.

Would Blood Fell erupt, Etna-like, and pour molten lava into the slaughtering sheds and yards of Geo. Drawbridge and Sons, High Class Butchers, Licensed for Game, and thence into the rest of Cronkley?

Would the legendary Cronkleydale Bore rush up the valley, destroying all in its path including the King Edward VII Memorial Swings?

Would the Cubberthwaite Fault, inexplicably ignored by generations of seismologists, suddenly slip and rend open the countryside from Thirsk to Kettlewell? No. Probably not. But the Man from Mars could hardly keep his Eucryl Smokers' Toothpowder on his brush as he thought of what might be, today, and tomorrow.

The second half of this cataclysmic double-header would be Cronkley -v- Garthrigg How in Sunday's Final of the Scallion Plate. First, there was the pre-ordained Saturday fixture at Cronkley, in the Nippon Missionary 4WD Fellside League, between the two very same teams!

The odds were on two Cronkley victories, and every platitude about cups being great levellers and cricket being a funny old game failed to change the opinion of all betting persons in Cronkley and many in Garthrigg How. Their combined enthusiasm for a winning double had forced the betting shop in Barnard Castle to make a special book on the issue.

Saturday's match at its beginning would have brought a smile to the bookie's face, had he been there. George Cartmell, belying his status as a notified Ancient Monument, leaped yards to his right to catch Cronkley star opener Hobson off Walker's seventh delivery. Banks bowled Shirley soon after, scoring became nigh impossible, and on 20 overs the high-chinned ones were a mere 25 for 2. Everton and Chivers soldiered on, the former sending everybody to sleep while the latter woke everybody up with his loud comments on his own stroke play.

"Bad shot!" he would cry, as he punished the air. "Bad shot again!

What are you playing at?"

The agony was over when Chivers hit an uppish drive and Metcalf, doing his usual impersonation of a policeman in a coma on point duty, stuck up his right hand as a stop sign and found the ball in it.

A flurry at the end from Shaw got Cronkley over the hundred, but Garthrigg How skipper Satterdyke enjoyed his tea enormously, seeing a league and cup double beckoning him and his team to unimaginable fame, possibly even a photograph in the *Northern Echo*.

113 wanted off 45, that's only two and a half an over. *Niet problyema*. Alas for the hopes of men. Satterdyke opened with confidence but was feeling distinctly queasy after watching his first four partners go for a total of 27 after scraping through 22 overs.

He and Halliday did a bit, but then Shaw bowled a straight one, Satterdyke decided to get them in sixes, and total collapse ensued.

In the pavilion afterwards was gloom and despondency, and some education. "Oh, the ignomony" said Satterdyke, a school teacher. "What's ignomony?" asked Metcalf.

"It's Stage Three" responded Naylor. "First you get pocket money, then you get matrimony, then you get ignomony. See?"

The Man from Mars, outside the door, opined to nobody that Satterdyke had got too excited and thus missed his opportunity. He had, in fact, failed to strike while the stitch was hot.

Satterdyke picked up his kitbag and headed for the clubhouse bar, quoting (without realising it) from Isaiah XXII xiii: "Let us eat and drink; for tomorrow we shall die."

The Man from Mars headed for Cronkley market place pay-and-display launch-pad, quoting to himself from his other specialised subject, The American Novel 1930-1939.

"After all, tomorrow is another day" he said, and was gone with the wind.

Cronkley 112 for 6, Everton 44 n.o. Walker 3-30.
Garthrigg How 63. Shaw 5-23.
Cronkley 17pts, Garthrigg How 4pts

Great bear out-glittered by Garthrigg stars

Following the example of its illustrious progenitor, the Scallion Cup, the Plate final is a two-innings match on a neutral ground. The Cup final is, of course, played on Richmond's cultured turf; the Plate has to be played wherever, in this case at Great Cubberthwaite.

The first innings is 30 overs but fine judgement is required later since the second innings has no specific dividing line. This part of the match consists of 90 overs altogether, but if the side batting first is got out in 39, the other team has a potential 51 — or, the side going in first may declare at any time.

The draw, naturally, is not an option.

Cronkley were inserted by Sunday skipper Erickson who opened the bowling with the beastly boy Walker and McThunderbolt Cheyne. The Scottish fast bowler was complaining of a headache and, not wishing to over-extend himself in case he was needed later, was replaced by Murgatroyd. This proved to be an inspired move as the cheerful Neville, he of the six-foot body hung on a five-foot skeleton, plugged away and took five.

97 off 30 didn't look too bad, but at 27 for 2 off 14 Garthrigg How were well behind the rate. In came wrinkly hero Naylor who, after a circumspect start, carefully ran out Parks and then began to lay about him mightily.

With two sixes and a four off the last over, Naylor helped his team to a first innings lead of 31. Then, things began to go wrong. Hobson, first with Shirley and then with Bird, was untroubled and Erickson felt himself running out of options as the score mounted.

Cronkley had wiped off the lead and moved to 55 ahead and only 20 overs and one wicket were gone! In sheer desperation the skipper threw the ball to Naylor who, fielding at first slip, was being unbearable about his performance so far.

Of all teams, near neighbours Cronkley should surely be familiar by now with Naylor's curious whirlybird action but they played as if seeing it, or someone suffering from Non Specific Bowleritis, for the first time.

"They're crumbling like dominoes" observed the Man from Mars, enigmatically, and he was right.

With 50 overs gone and the score on 180 for 9, seven of them to Naylor, the Cronkley skipper had a choice. Declare, or be totally humiliated by Naylor. He chose discretion and set a target of 150 in 40 overs.

He was soon very happy as he watched Garthrigg How take their turn at crumbling. Asquith, Padgett, Parks, Satterdyke — all were gone as Halliday strode in to join Naylor with the score at 25. Halliday, wide of rib-cage, bicep and smile, immediately showed Cronkley where the boundary is at Great Cubberthwaite. Naylor, fearing that he might be eclipsed, very nearly succeeded in showing them where the boundary started over the beck at Garthrigg How.

At 93 for 4 and with their opposition dangerously back on course, Cronkley held an in-depth team discussion. Halliday, trying to listen, thought he heard the phrase "straight one" float out from the huddle and waited with some trepidation — justified, as it turned out.

His replacement was Erickson who watched in dismay as Naylor padded up and offered no stroke to a ball on middle stump, then walked out inspecting the edge of his bat. In came Dobber Metcalf and the two batted as if they couldn't bear the thought of what Naylor would say if the match was lost. By the time they'd gone, both caught behind in the same over, the task was just 13 wanted off two overs, with two wickets to fall.

That one of the wickets was Walker's at number 11 was pointed out forcefully to Cheyne and the venerable Cartmell by their skipper, and Cheyne set out to show that Bannockburn wasn't the only fixture in which the Scots could vanquish the English.

He hit two fours. Cartmell nudged two singles. Cheyne hit an obvious single but called for the second, forgetting that Cartmell by now would we unable to hear through his own heaving breath.

148 for 9. Last man in. Three balls left. Walker knew what to do. He had been told by Naylor. As the bowler came into his delivery stride, Walker ran towards him holding his bat straight in front of himself. He meant to drop the ball dead in the middle of the pitch, but missed it and was stranded. The keeper, in panic, threw at the stumps and also missed. The batsmen ran one.

Cartmell to face. Scores tied. Tension unbearable. There was much discussion among the Cronkley boys but finally they had to bowl it.

As the Man from Mars observed later, it was so quiet you could have heard a mouse drop.

Walker, backing up, set off running as soon as he was legally entitled and just kept going regardless. Cartmell did one of his little nurdles towards backward square leg and set off likewise but at a slower rate.

Walker came rushing in, his bat grounded in front of him as he had been taught by Naylor. The fielder picked up the ball and was about to throw to the bowler who could have run Cartmell out easily, when he froze, transfixed.

The toe of Walker's bat hit the bowlers' footmarks and stopped dead. Walker kept going, lost his grip, and felt a crushing pain as the bat handle shot into his box. For a moment he was airborne, horizontal, like a sky-diver before his chute opens, pivoting on his bat by a private, plastic-protected fulchrum.

As his momentum carried him over the crease and he crashed to the ground, the panting Cartmell arrived at the far end and Garthrigg How, by outstanding team effort, had beaten the brightest constellation in the dale and had won the Scallion Plate.

Cronkley 97-7. Murgatroyd 5-37; & 180-9, Hobson 68. Naylor 7-49. Garthrigg How 128-3, Naylor 63 n.o; & 150-9, Halliday 36, Naylor 35, Erickson 26, Metcalf 25.

Satterdyke grits, umpire quits

Nobody seemed to mind that Saturday's league match against Great Cubberthwaite was rained off, thus preventing another certain league victory. The glow from *La Triomphe Magnifique*, as Satterdyke kept calling it, still illuminated the embers of the soul and Garthrigg How's more literary players could say "Great Cubberthwaite? Pshaw! A mere bagatelle", and Dobber Metcalf could say something similar.

Now, to help the lads float more gently back to earth, whither should point the questing bonnet of Cecil Hardwick's minibus, also Light Removals, but towards the home of the Perambulators?

These gentlemen, all tending towards the Rover and the BMW rather than the Toyota pick-up, are members of the professions in their working lives but are distinctly and purely amateur when it comes to cricket. Many have been privately educated and speak articulately about their own cricket, and so it is always a pleasure to meet them.

Usually, this fixture does not extend the abilities of Garthrigg How, even when playing on the grammar school pitch that Perambulators hire as their home, but today skipper Erickson was without some of his best men. He had even been forced to call up Clunk Metcalf again and so a safety-first policy of No Prisoners was ordered in place of the usual gentle mickey take.

Yesterday's rain had made the pitch extra sporting and Perambulators' captain Clockstein was hit about the person many times as he dragged his way into double figures.

This was starting to get worrying. More attack was required, and so Erickson moved the fearless Satterdyke to silly mid on and the impervious Clunk to forward short square.

Asquith, unfortunate in his imbalance between brain and ability, responded with two full length balls outside off stump. Erickson had a word.

"One. This man Clockstein is an author, an admirable thing in its way, and he is widely respected in the small and secret world of palaeobotany" he said to the eagerly listening Asquith. "Two. He also reads. He has read the chapter of a book about cricket which deals with front-foot play. Three. Please note the fielders stationed close to the bat on the leg side."

Asquith nodded, charged in, and sent down a truly bowel-easing bouncer.

Naylor helpfully pointed out that there were three insurance brokers in his team should Clockstein wish to revise his cover, and Satterdyke and Metcalf moved in two paces.

Clockstein froze in terror at the next ball, was bowled middle peg, and resistance was meagre after that — so meagre, in fact, that Clunk Metcalf was put on to bowl.

The Sunday skipper, presumably, was expecting Metcalf's donkey droppings to give encouragement and succour to the dregs of the Perambulators' batting, but no such luck.

The umpire at Clunk's end, a retired loss adjuster, walked off the field in a huff when Clunk gave him a quarter bottle of brandy to hold, and his replacement from among the retired batsmen stayed only for two balls while both his remaining colleagues took early retirement also.

With such a pitiful target to beat, Leader Erickson decided to fiddle with his arrangements and put his men in backwards.

Nobody appreciated the fine opportunity thus presented and Garthrigg How were soon 24 for 5. Grit was required, and it came in the form of Satterdyke.

Eschewing the habits of a lifetime — run the other chap out, then get caught at mid on — wily Wayne bent sternly to his task and with Parks already batting in character a win was taken one run at a time.

Perambulators 55, Clockstein 28. Asquith 4-11, Metcalf 2-0. Garthrigg How 58-6, Satterdyke 20 n.o.

Garsserigg 'ow, un point

Times have changed at Barrowmoor. Such high fellside hamlets were always considered too small and remote for very much cricket. Even when motor transport and the league game came to that distant terminus in 1949, in the shape of The Fellside Conference and Cecil Hardwick's very first second-hand Plaxton's 32-seater, there was a row about the pitch.

Wilfrid Baynes, the farmer who owned the field, became convinced that a certain member of the cricket team was doing rather more to his wife than teaching her the piano. Mr Baynes therefore would wait until a match started on a Saturday, and then go down there with half a dozen Swaledales and a sheepdog.

He would lean on the gate with the animals all calmly beside him, then as soon as the piano teacher came in to bat or came on to bowl, he would open the gate, whisper "Go by" to the dog, and play would have to be suspended.

With two low whistles of instruction the dog would gather the sheep neatly on the strip and lie down. The sheep, being Swaledales, would form an outward-facing phalanx, leave their deposits centrally and dig up many divots with their stamping feet.

Wilf would call them back after a while, but his point was made, and it was his field . . .

After three such incidents the grandees of The Fellside Conference asked for an assurance from Barrowmoor CC that no more matches would be posted as "No Result — sheep". The cricket captain (not the piano teacher) had a word with Wilfrid and was able to so assure the worried men at League HQ. Next home game, Wilfrid released six Fresian bull calves and there was no more league cricket there until modern times, the Nippon Missionary 4WD sponsorship and the Barrowmoor sports centre.

Commander Websdale RN (ret'd.) has assumed the captaincy since the Garthrigg How game earlier in the season and has attracted to his team another senior sportsman late of Her Majesty's armed forces, a former pilot with CrabAir, Squadron Leader McCabe.

These two clearly regarded Garthrigg How as so many mean and lowly pongos and brown jobs. They opened the home batting with disdain and, it has to be said, fully justified confidence.

No matter what skipper Satterdyke tried, and no matter how wily his moves, nothing came of it except the tea interval.

The total looked to be in reach, even remembering what Websdale had done earlier in the season with his innocent-looking spinners.

There was, as it happened, no need for spinners, free from sin or otherwise, since the brothers Abel, humorously named Leonard and Brough by their parents, found no difficulty whatsoever in parting the full complement of Garthrigg How batsmen from their wickets in just under the hour.

It was vintage hang-glider Cartmell who squirted the vital run past gully which brought the single batting point, thus preventing the shame of equalling Norway's performance in this year's Eurovision Song Contest.

Barrowmoor 127-0, Websdale 53 n.o, McCabe 71 n.o.
Garthrigg How 41. L.Abel 6-14. B.Abel 4-24.
Barrowmoor 18pts, Garthrigg How 1pt.

SUNDAY AUGUST 26

Under the spreading chestnut tree

One day in the early summer a chap walked into The Wintering Hogg who turned out to be the landlord of a pub called The Pigeon Pie in Thorpe Scawby, about 20 miles away.

Discussion turned to cricket, and examples of the landed gentry taking an interest in cricket, and before too many pints were consumed a date had been made. A Garthrigg How XI, for the day representing The Wintering Hogg, would play A Pigeon Pie Select XI, on Scawby Hall's private ground.

Scawby Hall's private ground isn't like Garthrigg Hall's, however. It is not regularly used, it has very long undergrowth around the edges and, most curiously, it is on two levels, one ten feet above the other, joined by a steeply sloping bank running the full length of the field on a line parallel to the pitch and at the distance where square leg (or old fashioned point) usually is.

Umpires tend not to go to that side at all, but fielders have the choice, if they are thereabouts, of standing at the top of the bank ready to run down, or at the bottom of the bank ready to turn and run up.

Garthrigg How had included a few irregulars, to try and balance what they guessed might be a gap in class (O, arrogance!). Lady Marjory herself was going to play but at the last minute decided to be umpire instead.

On the Pigeon Pie side was a man who must have been the village blacksmith, a massive figure whose huge chest and belly were tightly covered in a galleon-sail of flannel shirt, a shirt so dirty that it was polished to a reflective ink-black at that point where person would meet mahogony when leaning against the bar. Erickson made a mental note to check the Pigeon Pie bar later, to see if he could spot the blacksmith's regular place.

Also in the team, all of whose members walked out to the middle to watch the toss, was the Yorkshire Dales National Park peripatetic village idiot — Thorpe Scawby's turn this week, obviously — and the Thorpe Scawby village dwarf. Dobber Metcalf said he was going to whack the ball into the long grass near wherever the dwarf happened to be fielding, so he could watch the grass tops wave as the little fellow looked for it.

The Pigeon Pie won the toss and elected to bat and, despite the generosity of the Marchioness of Keld, were 11 for 5 in minutes.

In came the blacksmith, a fine thread of blue smoke finding its way past his family-size features from the roll-up which dangled at his bottom lip. Skipper Erickson's instinct was to pass an instruction around his fielders, but he decided it was unnecessary and he was proved right.

A widish, slow long hop arrived from Donald Davies. The blacksmith took an almighty swing which, had he connected properly, would have sent the ball through the window of Men's Surgical Ward, Richmond Hospital, 25 miles away. Instead of this expected and universally hoped for result, there was a distinct snick off the top edge and the ball plopped into stand-in keeper Macdonald's gloves.

Silence. Nobody appealed. Macdonald tossed the ball underarm to square leg (at the bottom of the bank) who tossed it to mid on, who returned it to Davies.

Not a throat was cleared, not a smile was allowed to dilute the seriousness of the moment.

The blacksmith, sure that some kind of cricketing mickey was being taken, puffed on his roll-up and settled with a fierce glare into a crouching stance ready for the next ball.

"Under the spreading chestnut tree, the village smithy stands" whispered her Ladyship to Batman as he walked past her to his mark. Pondering this, and wondering if it was the first words of a different version of a joke he knew about six virgins and a horse shoe, Davies lolloped in and provided another gentle long hop.

The blacksmith took a tremendous heave, a heave so vigorous that his roll-up fell out, but no contact was made between bat and ball. The latter, undisturbed in its slow flight, struck the blacksmith on the foot as it attempted its second bounce.

Davies, forgetting himself, turned to Lady Marjory and, with arms raised, cried "Ow!". Lady Marjory quelled the rest of the appeal with an imperious stare and said "Not out!" just in case.

It didn't matter, as it happened, because the ball rolled from the blacksmith's size 12 black slip-on, onto the leg stump, dislodging a bail.

The blacksmith knew what this meant and walked off with the bat over his shoulder, pausing only to pick up his cigarette.

The rest of the cricket can be passed over, as indeed can the later sight of Barry Naylor, sliding down the wall of The Pigeon Pie saying that his was a double vodka and Russian and he'd had several.

Her Ladyship can never be passed over and was instrumental in an occurrence of such outstanding bravery that it must surely be a prime candidate for Moment of the Year.

Frank Smailes, the quiet and unassuming (he has to be) husband of Belinda the She-Dragon, and therefore the nominal landlord of The Wintering Hogg, was partnering the Marchioness in a game of pool, hoping to restore his sporting reputation after dropping two catches and being out first ball. Their opponents were the peripatetic village idiot and the blacksmith.

The game was virtually over. All the blacksmith had to do was pot his last colour, which was sitting over a pocket, and then pot the black, which was sitting over another.

Before these final shots were taken, the village idiot decided to get them in, and the blacksmith decided to go through a door at the back of the bar to search beneath his corporation for whatever physical interface he maintained between his bladder and the outside world.

While they were away, Lady Marjory looked at Frank Smailes, and then looked at the black ball. Frank's face fell. Not on your Nelly, his eyes seemed to say. Come along, don't be such a weed, Lady Marjory's eyes replied. Frank, who went to school at Giggleswick, whispered in Lady Marjory's ear.

> *"The smith, a mighty man is he,*
> *With large and sinewy hands;*
> *And the muscles of his brawny arms*
> *Are strong as iron bands."*

Lady Marjory smiled. She had been to school at somewhere even better than Giggleswick.

"It's as you say, O Frankie dear,
A barn door, front and back.
Now prove you're either man or mouse
*And move the ****ing black!"*

Taking a deep breath, Frank moved the black. The idiot came back with the drinks — two pints of bitter, a pint of lager and a large Wood's and ginger wine for the Marchioness — and the blacksmith came back from the loo. He picked up his cue and bent to the white ball, expecting to see his last colour waiting at the pocket's mouth for any kind of touch to send it in.

Instead, he saw he was impossibly snookered by the black. He grunted. He straightened up and scratched his head. He looked at Lady Marjory, but she was deep in conversation with Frank about a fell pony that a gypsy was trying to sell her.

The blacksmith consulted his own partner, the Yorkshire Dales National Park peripatetic village idiot, who didn't understand the question. With no alternative, the blacksmith played the black with a nothing shot, Lady Marjory potted her colours and then the black as necessary, and Garthrigg How were able to complete an evening of total victory, including cricket, darts, dominoes and pool.

The Pigeon Pie, Thorpe Scawby, 16.
The Wintering Hogg 18-4.

SATURDAY SEPTEMBER 1

Tooth-skin unscathed in great escape

How long ago it now seems that the oracle saw porkers in the sky and Garthrigg How's first league victory was grasped from an incredulous Crosby Hawker team.

That same team, now top of the league and fully expecting Higher Things next year, was in no mood to repeat the experience when visiting the graceful environs of Garthrigg Hall.

Garthrigg How, in a familiar role as the Houdini or possibly the Tommy Cooper of the Nippon Missionary 4WD Fellside League Division 3, needed to win to be sure of staying up. Losing would probably mean relegation unless Fingby and Sowerby Rudd both also lost, which was unlikely as they were playing each other.

If Sowerby Rudd won and Garthrigg How lost, that was it. If Fingby won, it would mean three teams on very similar total numbers of points, and so it would depend on the day's extras for batting and bowling.

Banks had done well in the previous fixture with his straight bananas, and so wily skipper Satterdyke opened with him at one end and the Scottish fast bowler at the other.

Banks bowled opener Garrett with his second ball, but not much happened after that apart from arm-stretching by the umpire at the Lady Marjory's Conservatory end, indicating that Banks was moving the ball away from the bat.

Meanwhile Cheyne was having no luck at all and the skipper had to take him off before the very last strands from an already scantily clad pate were wrenched out in frustration.

The batsmen, trying to memorise several new (to them) Scottish terms of abuse in case they never played Garthrigg How again, completely forgot to pay attention to the doom-laden grenades lobbed up by Padgett. This time-warped old fox caught and bowled both of them, then Banks got two, and 67 for 4 was not as intended by the lofty visitors.

Satterdyke's inspiration had almost run its course, however. Craven and Mills came together, pushed a few singles and their luck, and then launched an aerial bombardment which had Garthrigg men scattering, arms outstretched in supplication.

The captain, seeing the overs disappearing, realising that he wasn't going to win, decided that Crosby Hawker had better get as many runs as possible so that, in chasing them, Gathrigg How might get more batting points. So he put Naylor and Erickson on.

Erickson understood what his captain wanted and obliged with four overs for 39. Naylor preferred a more direct approach and took four wickets.

In reply, Padgett and Halliday put on 51 before Halliday missed a straight one. Padgett, in Satterdykian mood, tested the catching talents of almost all the fielders (and found them wanting) but the score grew and grew.

Harwood came on to bowl his military medium, irritatingly accurate stuff and took four wickets in three overs.

The match situation, as R Benaud calls it, was as follows after 30 overs of the second half:

Crosby Hawker 219-8. Garthrigg How 99-5.
Points so far: Crosby Hawker 7, Garthrigg How 6.

The Man from Mars pointed out that another 61 runs would give us eight points which, according to his gamma-particle swing-ometer, would be enough unless Sowerby Rudd won, or Fingby won in a high-scoring game.

This fascinating and revealing information was greeted in silence by the having- and not-yet-batted Garthrigg men.

With Parks, Davies and Satterdyke gone it could have been argued, and indeed was, that there was little left in the way of batting. Murgatroyd was determined to show them something different and, with a complete lack of respect for the bowling which had troubled more elevated colleagues, increased Garthrigg momentum almost to 'surge' status. Nobody ever thought that 219 was feasible, except Murgatroyd. Certainly Erickson never did, not until they passed 200 and he'd got back all of the 39 he'd given away while bowling.

Alas for the Sunday skipper he was not to see the glory, for of a sudden he received one which, as he later related, moved half a yard in the air one way, six inches the other off the pitch and kept low.

Naylor, like Murgatroyd, was unable to find any such subtlety and deceit in the Crosby Hawker bowling. The league leaders could not believe what was happening, and said so.

The Man from Mars had left his Frequency Modulated Data Interceptor in the saucer and so was forced to consult a more pedestrian medium of earthling communications, last week's *Cronkleydale Mercury*.

It would seem that if Cronkley, playing at Gallinglath, and Nuncotes, at home to High Hutton, both had good wins then a losing Crosby Hawker, instead of being champions, might only be third!

This is the time when you need a cool headed Leader. Instead Crosby Hawker appeared to have a parliament of rooks, and Naylor was enjoying telling them how much he was looking forward to playing them again next year.

The next-to-last over summed it all up, with Garthrigg How needing 11 to win, and Crosby needing four wickets. It began with two wides, which Naylor ignored, a straight one and another wide. Eight to win, off 11 balls.

A single to deep square. Four more left in the over. Huge appeal for caught behind off a ball which Murgatroyd never saw, much less touched. A single to third man. Naylor takes massive swipe at ball a foot outside off stump, which then soars almost vertically into air. They run two while Crosby Hawker fielders blame each other for not catching it. Naylor blocks last ball of over, deciding that Murgatroyd deserves chance of being out and so letting somebody else score winners.

Murgatroyd, his indefatigable spirit shining through all difficulties, faced the first of the last. It was fastish and shortish, and he tonked it over deep mid wicket for six.

And so it was that Garthrigg How did the double over Crosby Hawker, thus accounting for 66.6% of their league wins this season.

Crosby Hawker 219-8, Craven 61, Mills 55. Naylor 4-18.
Garthrigg How 221-6, Padgett 48, Murgatroyd 48 n.o, Erickson 39.
Gathrigg How 19pts, Crosby Hawker 8pts.

Fingby beat Sowerby Rudd and so those two teams go down to Division 4. Cronkley lost to Gallinglath and so Nuncotes are this year's Division 3 Champions, with Crosby Hawker second.

Stricken by post-security syndrome

Traditionally the last Sunday friendly of the season is against Darguesby who, regarding it as the second half of their village fete week-end, bring a coachload of spectators.

They all require tea and always get tea, even though it means the Garthrigg How team has to take its tea in the pub car park.

This year there was to be a bonus. Belinda the She-Dragon, who never drinks, was persuaded on Saturday night to take a glass of hock in honour of the cricket team's victory over Crosby Hawker and the consequent assurance of matches next year against Cronkley and Great Cubberthwaite.

As always with someone who never drinks, one glass became several and Belinda became a martyr to Post-Security Syndrome, or PSS.

Most of the team were PSS as well, but one or two were also mentally agile enough to get the in-cups Belinda to promise a barrel of beer for the match tomorrow.

News of this unheard-of generosity was all around the North Dales Triangle the next morning and there was a fair crowd at the beer table at Garthrigg Hall by 2.30pm on Sunday.

When 2.45pm came, some of the players decided they had better have some of the beer before it all went.

When 3pm came, and there was still no sign of the Darguesby coach, Erickson organised a whip-round to replace the empty barrel.

The sun shone with increasing hotness. People lay around in care-less postures. Lady Marjory told the vicar the one about the lady novelist and the lobster. Belinda eventually agreed with Dobber Metcalf that Tuesday was market day in London, providing he would run round to the pub and fetch a bottle of hock.

At 3.35pm precisely, the Fixture Secretary, sipping her first hock of the day, had a blinding realisation. She had discussed the one-sidedness

of their relationship with the Darguesby skipper last year, and for the first time in 20 years the match for this season had been arranged at their ground.

Belinda the She-Dragon was wondering how she could reveal this information while retaining her fault-free image when Satterdyke thought to look at his fixture card. Later it was decided that a cricket match without the cricket can be a very enjoyable social occasion.

SUNDAY SEPTEMBER 9

Time travellers zap village

Tears of nostalgia clouded the vision of Garthrigg How skipper Satterdyke as he watched heroes of the past stride to the wicket on behalf of Club President Marjory, Marchioness of Keld, in the traditional end-of-season fixture.

First came the stately Gilbert Crane, a man of grand stature and slow motion whose bat, carbon-dated to the late Bronze Age, is the colour of Bisto. This is not the only relationship between Crane and gravy, of course, since he has made lots of it in his life and now runs between the wickets as if up to his thighs in it.

With him was Alec Woodbridge, still looking very young for his age — presumably the back-in-time journey to Garthrigg How from Leeds in his Tardis SRi had taken years off him.

These two stars from Old Garthrigg How's Greatest Hits coped nonchalantly with the current village attack, more intent perhaps on enjoying their physical return to the fields of their youth than in scoring a great many runs.

Guest comic Danny Banks, twin brother of Barry, did a quick turn when Crane was run out, causing the Man from Mars to wonder where Barry had got such splendid new kit from.

He clearly enjoys this annual encounter, the Man from Mars, perhaps because it is so rare for him to be in the society of other non-terrestrial and fourth-dimensional beings, or perhaps because it usually proves, as he so often says, that the men of yesterday were so much better at cricket than the men of today.

When Banks was replaced by Steve Royd and Woodbridge by Erickson, things livened up even more. Once again this season Erickson, qualifying for the President's XI through age, had the experience of scoring half a dozen runs while his partner scored at ten times that rate.

Steve's brother Glynn then took over the massacre, causing the Lady Marjory to send in appreciation to The Wintering Hogg for another nine gallon barrel of Old Speckled Cock.

Satterdyke remained optimistic at tea time. Were not the majority of the President's men grey-bearded and thick-waisted?

In the field, surely they would be as statues, or at best only lumbering after the ball while Wayne's fit young fellows zipped at speed up and down the pitch.

This theorem might have been demonstrated had any of the Garthrigg men actually laid a bat on the ball. Instead they were destroyed by the burly Yorkshire Dales National Park Regional Convenor for CAMRA, Stewart Cammish, who was benefiting hugely from Lady Marjory's largesse in the Speckled Cock department.

He bounced in on his usual 11-stride, 30-yard run-up, stopped at the wicket as usual, turned his five-acre chest sideways and, as usual, delivered the ball at lightning speed.

With the village on 21 for 5 the President's locum as captain, the Most Venerable George Cartmell, took pity and put his grandson Darren on to bowl at one end, while Erickson puttered at the other.

Nobody on the village side could stand the thought of getting out to Erickson and so the generous gesture rather backfired. Instead of piling on the runs they blocked and pushed, making the Man from Mars remark that the bowling must be a lot more difficult out there than it looked from here.

Suddenly, the President's captain's grandson pulled a tin of spinach from his pocket and, crying "A-doddle-adump-a-dum" ran in to bowl with renewed vigour, thinking that was what his grandad wanted him to do. In five minutes Garthrigg How went from 43 for 5 to 59 for 9.

Enter Walker, The Beast. He scored two runs in completely different ways and then it was all over for another year.

President's XI 173-4, S Royd 63, Woodbridge 38.
Garthrigg How 61. Cammish 4-11, D Cartmell (aged 15) 4-6.

Garthrigg How CC

Results (last season)

Date	Opponent	Result
Sun April 29	Scallion Cup	
	1st Round: Kirkby Wathwell	L
Sat May 5	High Hutton	L
Sun May 6	Middleham Trophy 1st:	
	Swale Electricity	L
Sat May 12	Nuncotes	NR
Sun May 13	Long Asby	NR
Sat May 19	Fingby	L
Sun May 20	Les Cigalles de Harrogate	W
Sat May 27	Gallinglath	L
Sun May 28	Scallion Plate 1st	
	Great Cubberthwaite	W
Sat Jun 2	Sowerby Rudd	NR
Sun Jun 3	Perambulators	W
Sat Jun 9	Cronkley	L
Sun Jun 10	Scallion Plate 2nd	
	Netherclough	W
Sat Jun 17	Great Cubberthwaite	L
Sun Jun 18	Buttle	NR
Sat Jun 24	Barrowmoor	L
Sun Jun 25	Scallion Plate 3rd	
	Staggerthorpe Res.	W
Sat Jun 30	Crosby Hawker	W
Sun Jul 1	Sunbiggin	W
Sat Jul 7	High Hutton	NR
Sun Jul 8	Milk Marketers	NR
Sat Jul 14	Nuncotes	L
Sun Jul 15	Scallion Plate Semi-final:	
	Little Battisford	W
Sat Jul 21	Fingby	W
Sun Jul 22	Buttle	W
Sat Jul 28	Gallinglath	NR
Sun Jul 29	Fellside Young Farmers	D
Sat Aug 4	Sowerby Rudd	L
Sun Aug 5	Ravenstone	L
Sat Aug 11	Cronkley	L
Sun Aug 12	Scallion Plate	
	Final: Cronkley	W
Sat Aug 18	Great Cubberthwaite	NR
Sun Aug 19	Perambulators	W
Sat Aug 25	Barrowmoor	L
Sun Aug 26	Pigeon Pie	W
Sat Sep 1	Crosby Hawker	W
Sun Sep 2	Darguesby	NR
Sun Sep 9	President's XI	L

Cronkleydale Mercury

The voice of the Northern Dales since 1827   *Saturday 15th September* **30p**

CLAIMING DATES

Tuesday 18 Sept
Cronkley YFs/Rotary, Blood Fell Yomp

Sunday 23 Sept
Gt Cubberthwaite VH, Car Treasure Hunt

Thursday 4 Oct
Buttle VH, Snr Citz Merry Neet

Monday 15 Oct
Barrowmoor WI, Bring, Buy and Borrow

Friday 19 Oct
Cronkley Market Hall
Dog Show and Concert by Cubberstones Chorale

Thursday 25 Oct
Garthrigg Hall (Top Wood)
Garthrigg How WI and guest White Magic Demo

Friday 5 Nov
Gt Cubberthwaite FC, Bonfire and Fireworks.
BBQ by Brian 'Blacksmoke' Nidderton

Thursday 18 Nov
Waxby VH, Doms and Beetles

Saturday Nov 24
The Wintering Hogg Inn, Annual dinner —
cricket club

Thursday December 13
The Wintering Hogg Inn, Christmas Dominoes

Thursday Dec 20
The Wintering Hogg Inn, Christmas Darts

Saturday Feb 10
Cronkley Market Hall, Ceilidh, Supper and
Indoor Sports, Garthrigg How CC

Sunday May 5
Garthrigg Hall, Car Boot Sale and Antiques Road Show.
Marchioness of Keld and Garthrigg How CC

Respected Cubberthwaite farmer dies

WILSON DOWLY, 69, of Looking Flatt, Great Cubberthwaite, died on Sunday suddenly, at home.

The funeral, at St Cuthbert's on Wednesday, was attended by large numbers. Six ex chairmen of Cronkley Show bore his coffin.

Mr Dowly was very well known in the area and was a leading light in the Northern Dales Rough Sheep Society.

In his youth he had captained both the football and cricket clubs and had trials for Huddersfield Town FC, then an important power in the Football League.

He served on the Committee of Cronkley Show for 40 years and was an Honorary Life Steward of the North Yorkshire Buffaloes as well as a past Provincial Grand Master of the Freemasons, based at Cronkley Lodge.

The vicar of Cubberthwaite-cum-Garthrigg, Rev. Luciwell, praised Mr Dowly's lifelong devotion to sheep breeding and suggested, in his now well accepted manner, that Wilson Dowly would no doubt be passing on a few tips to the Good Shepherd Himself.

Perhaps if God's ministers on earth possessed Wilson Dowly's ability at gathering, driving and penning, the churches would be full to bursting, said Rev. Luciwell.

Wilson Dowly is survived by his wife Ena, sons Walter and Weston and daughter Elizabeth.

Women in the Community

CRONKLEY

Cronkley celebrated their 50th Anniversary and organised a special party to which former members were invited. The oldest founder member present was Mrs Nancy Murchison, 89, who looked in very fine fettle.

A home-made buffet was enjoyed, including vols au vent and quiches by Mesdames Bullock and Douglas, home cured ham and salted beef by Mrs Devine, and Bulgar wheat salad with Japanese raw fish by Ms Griffiths.

Mrs Eglinton made gold silk buttonholes for all members and guests, who included two representatives from the North Riding Executive Committee, Mrs Norma Slater and Mrs Thelma Minsceough.

The raffle was won by Mrs Tomlinson, who was very pleased to receive a 42 lb pumpkin grown by Ms Griffiths. The competition for a table mat resulted: 1 Ms Griffiths, 2 Mrs Bullock, 3 Mrs Douglas.

GREAT CUBBERTHWAITE

The President Mrs Cowper opened the meeting at which there were 13 present. Mrs Foulthwick introduced the speaker, Mrs Valerie Saxon-Zimber from Romaldskirk, who gave a very interesting talk on "The Hedgerows of Switzerland", illustrated with slides.

Mrs Brunskill thanked the speaker and was pleased on behalf of the members to accept Mrs Saxon-Zimber's offer of a talk next season on "Cheese making in Switzerland in the 1920s", illustrated with her own sketches.

Mrs Nelson gave notice of the annual outing on the 3rd of October to Bridlington and Flamborough Head, and then The Stephen Joseph Theatre in the Round, Scarborough.

The competition for a tablet of soap had a disappointing entry and so an extempore limerick competition was organised and resulted: 1 Mrs Brunskill, 2 Mrs Cowper, 3 Mrs Dowdeswell.

GARTHRIGG HOW

In the absence of the President, Lady Marjory, the Secretary Mrs Naylor opened the meeting and gave notice of the outing to the High Force Hotel, Teesdale, for lunch and a conducted tour around the new brewery.

Mrs Novotny as Special Organiser gave notice of the Casino Night at The Hall, by invitation only. Mrs Novotny will be approaching some of the local WIs.

Mrs Halliday introduced the guest, Mr Robert Snelgrove, a tutor at Darlington College of Art, who demonstrated "Calligraphy with Quill and Brush".

Members were given the opportunity to make red and black ink, and to sharpen quills with a Victorian silver pen knife.

Mrs Cartmell thanked the guest, adding that ready-made ink and fountain pens were available for sale at the post office and stores, use it or lose it.

The competition for a small decorative tin resulted: 1 Mrs Jellicoe, 2 Mrs Cartmell, 3 Mrs Novotny.